PRAISE FOR HA
AND THREE DEGREES OF LAW

"Harlan York is a Street Fighter."

> - GARRY KASPAROV
> *Greatest Chess Player of All Time*

"Harlan York is a true professional who cares about his clients and his work."

> - *PETER RONO*
> *Olympic Gold Medalist*

"I have been teaching for over twenty years and often ask law students what do they want out of their legal careers. To be honest, most respond with very vague answers. I encourage them to take some time during (if not before) law school to really talk with attorneys about their daily work lives. Harlan York's book jump starts that process. It pulls back the curtain on some of the ways lawyers spend their times. Much more realistic than Television or Film, read this engaging book to take a peek into the legal world."

> - LENNI BENSON
> *Safe Passage Project Director, New York Law School; American Immigration Lawyers Association National Award Winner, Outstanding Professor Of Immigration Law*

"Harlan York is knowledgeable, articulate and very, very helpful."

- JOE LYNN TURNER

Former Vocalist for Deep Purple and Rainbow

"Harlan York's story is of a lawyer whose personal values gracefully align with his professional values as a lawyer. That alignment is the foundation for high-performance, ethical lawyering. As a teacher of attorney ethics, his story represents the highest form of practice. His clients have reaped the benefit of a lawyer who is committed to them as individuals and who is determined to apply his creativity and expertise to their cause. Readers of Three Degrees of Law will reap the lessons of his story."

- MEG REUTER

Professor, Indiana University-Maurer Law School

Center on the Global Legal Profession

"Essential advice for all attorneys seeking to transform their 'job' into something more meaningful, a legal 'vocation.'"

- GABRIEL KAHN

Professor of Professional Practice, University of Southern California

Annenberg School for Communication and Journalism

"Many times Harlan York offered me sound advice in my personal and professional life and gave me great legal guidance. Harlan York is a straight shooter who tells it like it is."

- JAY HAYES
Brazilian Jiu Jitsu Champion

"Harlan York is the consummate professional. He shares an equal passion for the complexities and the very human aspects of law."

- JEREMY FREEMAN
Deadly Dragon Sound System, Reggae Genius

"After having horrendously fouled up my legal status, I was able to regain my status and now my American citizenship. For this, I fully credit Harlan York. I am certain Harlan York can help anyone."

- ALBERTO ARTASANCHEZ
Creator Of Visual Voice Mail
(Highest Revenue-Producing Application For Android Smartphones)

"I recommend everyone to Harlan York. He has a client for life with me, my business, and my family."

- WAYNE PRICE
Director Of Coaching, FC Sportika;
Former Pro Welsh Football Player

THREE DEGREES OF LAW

UNLOCKING THE SECRETS TO HAPPINESS

AND SUCCESS IN THE LEGAL UNIVERSE

By

HARLAN YORK

Published by Motivational Press, Inc.
1777 Aurora Road
Melbourne, Florida, 32935
www.MotivationalPress.com

Manufactured in the United States of America.

ISBN: 978-1-62865-162-1

Contents

ACKNOWLEDGEMENTS

Three Degrees of Law could not have become a reality without the help of the following people:

My editor, the incomparable Mark Eglinton

My publicist, the amazing Jennifer Prost

Justin Sachs and the other great people at Motivational

My outstanding associate attorneys: Lauren Anselowitz, Maggie Dunsmuir, Riki King and Mary Lynn Seery

Our great interns and staff

Most of all, my beautiful, brilliant wife, Beverly and our incredible children, Emily and Owen

In Memory of my Father, David "Duke" York

INTRODUCTION

Let me start with a confession. I'm dumb… Really dumb. Now, I know what you're thinking:

"This guy says he's dumb. It's a gimmick. He's full of it."

False modesty doesn't suit anyone, after all. But I'm serious. I actually am dumb. The key is—to paraphrase Edgar Bergen in his ventriloquist act (sampled by 3rd Bass on their album *The Cactus*)—"He is stupid, but he knows that he is stupid, and that almost makes him smart."

I'm going to repeat this so you understand exactly where I am going with it. I'm dumb, but I know I'm dumb, and that makes me smart.

Socrates similarly said, "The only true wisdom is in knowing you know nothing." I know that I don't know everything, and that alone makes me wise.

Here are a couple of examples to illustrate my point. Hand me a hammer and tell me to put a nail in a wall, and I will surrender to the task before I even try, because I know that the picture will end up crooked. If the copier breaks, forget calling me in to handle that problem. I'm about as useful as a caveman transported to our current world by time machine. I can't even make correct copies half of the time, let alone repair the machine that makes them.

But I know what I am good at...

With that in mind, this book is here to help lawyers, both young and old, as well as law students, undergraduates, and their parents. It is the byproduct of tens of thousands of hours spent practicing, studying, and speaking about the law.

Today, the legal profession is a difficult place to be. As of 2010, the American Bar Association counted more than 1.2 million lawyers in the United States along with over 145,000 law students.

This book is for them. It's also for anyone even thinking of going to law school, as well as their parents. And beyond the legal field, the guidance contained herein can be applied to a host of other industries outside of the law.

Think about what you are doing right now, whether you are a college kid or already attending law school; or if you are a young attorney, a longtime veteran of the legal wars, or right in the middle of your career.

Are you satisfied? Could you be better at whatever you are doing?

The answer is—no matter what—you can always improve.

I have been fortunate enough to enjoy my work, but I am never truly content.

And that's a good thing.

THE FIRST DEGREE

I Want to Be a Lawyer

———

Remember your first school play? In my case it was in kindergarten, where we made masks out of paper shopping bags and got on stage to say what we wanted to be when we grew up.

There were firemen and astronauts, of course, but I was the only one who actually came out and said the word "lawyer."

Heck, I didn't even know what an attorney did when I was five years old. All I knew is that they wore suits and ties and that my dad said I would be a good one when I finished school. He even told me that he would take me to Brooks Brothers one day to buy me a suit when I graduated, although back then I had no idea:

a. What Brooks Brothers was

b. My dad would never ever buy himself a suit there

I was standing on the stage with a paper mask, talking about how one day I would go to court and argue— apparently at age five I was already known for arguing well.

What the hell? It sounded good then.

A job versus a career

Many attorneys get up every day and grind it out, miserably. They have a job, but it's not one they like very much.

A 2010 survey of young lawyers conducted by The American Lawyer showed that job satisfaction had fallen to its lowest rate in six years. Of the associates polled at 124 firms, the satisfaction levels at 109 of them had dropped, and only 35 percent thought they even had a long-term future at their firms.

And what about those who did have a long-term future?

There's a great line in John Grisham's novel *The Associate*:

"I want to be a partner so I can sleep until 5:00 a.m. every day until I die at fifty. That's what I want."

The problem, I think, is that these people have a "job" mentality. It is not their fault; it's a belief system borne out of billable hours, demanding bosses, and unhappy clients. How can attorneys expect to be truly satisfied when they show up every day like assembly line workers who punch a clock every six minutes and don't get any enjoyment from the projects to which they are assigned?

My advice: choose a career—something more vocational with long-term prospects, and pick one that is satisfying. Select a working environment in which you can envision yourself *immersed*.

A friend of mine, Laura, did just this. She started out working on death penalty cases before moving on to federal criminal defense of all kinds. When I consider her passion for her work, it's when she refers to herself as a "sentencing geek" that I am most intrigued. Why? It reminds me of folks who love to keep score at ball games—except this is real life.

The truth is, Laura knows as much about the federal sentencing guidelines as any lawyer in America. It's her specialty, her area of expertise—her *career*, so much so that she can write and lecture about it to classes of law students and audiences of attorneys.

Another one of my buddies, Dave, did something equally stimulating with his law degree. He fell into intellectual property. For almost two decades, his career has been genuinely exciting. Dave has litigated some fascinating issues—cases that would make for compelling reading, even to those not particularly interested in the law.

But what do my two colleagues have in common? Well, they have chosen very specific areas—disciplines that are not based on just cranking out memoranda like zombies. No, these lawyers have taken on work that becomes a career. The way to find a career is to specialize, I have surmised, after twenty-something years of practicing in only one area.

Consider this:

» There are about 1.2 million lawyers in America.

» The percentage of practicing patent attorneys has consistently remained at approximately 1.5 percent; that represents about 18,000 patent lawyers in a nation of more than 311 million people.

» The National Academy of Elder Law Attorneys has around 4,200 members in the United States.

» The American College of Environmental Lawyers is a professional association of distinguished lawyers practicing in the field of environmental law. There are about 200 members.

» The First Amendment Lawyers Association has little more than 180 members. Its membership includes the most prominent First Amendment attorneys in the United States, covering virtually every state.

These are folks with careers, not jobs.

They find an area and devote themselves to it.

Some might even be dumb, but at least they know they're dumb.

Sleeping under the desk

I was talking to one of my associates about her old firm— where people worked 100 hours a week and slept under their desks. Suffice to say, she does not miss that lifestyle one bit.

Now, for some folks it may work, and more power to those of you who can actually do it. It's a warlike approach to law, some might argue. Some clients need soldiers to protect them, so if it works under those circumstances, who is anyone else to judge?

A lawyer who became a psychotherapist named Will Meyerhofer recalled his days at the law firm Sullivan & Cromwell in a blog post: "There's a machismo around staying up all night, night after night—like doing ten shots of tequila. You're tough.

Not a problem. With law firms' profits largely based on how many hours their lawyers bill, it's no surprise that most turn a blind eye to such behavior."

But that's a rough way to go for most folks, attorneys included. You don't have to be a doctor to know that a lack of sleep has deleterious effects on your health.

I have my own personal compromise when it comes to the need to get work done and also get a good night's sleep (and get some exercise, to boot).

Many nights, after my kids go to bed, I sit with my laptop on a recumbent bike, writing, answering client emails, and handling other work. I probably pedal ten miles while I type, then I get a good night's sleep.

A good night's sleep can do wonders for you and your clients. And as a parent, I extol the virtues of battling the urge to stay up late.

It goes back to the lessons we learn in kindergarten. A sound mind needs a sound body, and to get a sound body, one needs to sleep.

It does not matter where you work.

You have to get some sleep.

The Rick Ankiel method

For the baseball fans among you, this story will ring more than one bell. I use it as an example of how we can change roles in the law, sometimes quite drastically.

For those of you unfamiliar with Rick Ankiel, he was no Babe Ruth. However, the now-retired Ankiel was the first pro since Ruth—who had his heyday in the 1920s—to win ten games as a pitcher and hit fifty home runs.

Early on, he pitched very well for the St. Louis Cardinals and won the Rookie Pitcher of the Year Award from *The Sporting News*.

But to say Rick Ankiel lacked control is like saying the Empire State Building is a tall structure.

He struggled with the Cards for five years.

I was at the final National League 2000 playoff game in which he threw two of the nine wild pitches he accumulated against the New York Mets in three postseason appearances.

Later he went to the minors for a couple of seasons and reinvented himself as an outfielder. Ironically, he last appeared as a Met.

So, not only did Rick Ankiel go from ace pitcher to veteran outfielder but he did it on the other team. Thus I use Ankiel to make a point about radically switching one's function as an attorney.

What I am getting at here is that no matter what area of law you practice, if things are not going your way, you can reinvent yourself. You just need to capitalize on your strengths.

A few years back, I was coaching one of my kids' soccer teams. After one game, I met another dad who told me of how he had left big-time corporate law behind to open a small-town, one-attorney office. He had recreated himself. A new adventure had begun.

Endurance is your best hold

I will hazard a guess that most of you have never heard of Karl Gotch.

Under his real name, Charles Istaz, he wrestled for Belgium in the 1948 Olympics. Prior to that, he survived the Holocaust— as his German father refused to accept Nazi law, which resulted in parent and son being interned in a camp where they nearly starved to death.

Gotch made his living as a top pro wrestler (a common progression for former amateurs for decades) particularly in Japan, where he was dubbed "God of Wrestling."

In American pro wrestling he was considered old school, even in 1964, when he was quoted as saying, "My only disappointment is the strong reliance on gimmicks. I am at a disadvantage, because I don't dye my hair, I don't wear elaborate costumes, and I don't have any funny names for the holds I use. My only gimmick is a knowledge of wrestling."

What I admire most about Gotch is his famous work ethic. He was well known for saying, "Conditioning is your strongest hold."

Like so many other of my role models, Gotch influenced my dedication to my career as an attorney through his commitment to his sport.

Yet Gotch did not simply apply that approach to his athletic lifestyle. In his later years, when he had taken a hiatus from wrestling, he found himself in Hawaii. He needed work and found it as a sanitation man. "They'd get up at 4:30 or 5:00 in the morning, and he'd be running behind the truck, picking up garbage. He'd have the crew working out with him," said his tag team partner Rene Goulet.

Think about that for a second. Garbage men work damn hard. And here's this guy in his forties running behind a trash truck, throwing bags of refuse at full speed in the island heat, turning a "dirty job" into an exercise regimen.

The message? You take whatever you can get out of any work situation. Thus I found myself thinking of Gotch when I was a young lawyer, sitting in traffic approaching the George Washington Bridge. While the drivers around me angrily honked as they struggled through their morning commute, I tended to smile to myself, grateful that I had found work doing something I enjoyed and was apparently pretty good at.

Screw the traffic, I thought. *I will make the best of it*, I told myself, as I envisioned a former Olympian making the best out of a job in sanitation.

Speak another language

Studies have shown that one in every seven couples in America now identifies themselves as being in a mixed relationship. Whether we are talking race, religion, nationality, ethnicity, or some other major defining characteristic, our population is as diverse as it has ever been. I don't care if you practice international law or real estate; it is a great gift for any attorney to be able to speak more than one language.

I have found that my fluency in Spanish gives me a huge advantage when dealing with a large percentage of my client base. I am working on my Portuguese as well, and only wish I had studied more languages in high school.

Still, it is never too late. Nowadays, there are many ways to become conversant in other languages: Rosetta Stone, Pimsleur, as well as schools, tutors, or even just watching television on foreign language networks.

Also, be aware that you need not learn vocabulary in the same manner that a high school student does. Figure out the words most commonly used in your practice and focus on those. There is a good chance that you will never need to memorize lists of fruits and vegetables, but you clearly must know how to question a client about his tax history.

Many forecasts for the future consider various Chinese dialects as being extraordinarily useful for those who wish to be successful in business dealings—and for life in general. I wholeheartedly agree. I will start gently pushing my kids to pick up these skills before they reach adulthood. The overall life benefits can't be emphasized enough.

My buddy Tim is Greek; his wife Dina is Peruvian. Their child was trilingual as a preschooler. What a blessing in a world where the ability to speak a variety of languages opens many doors.

Nothing spells relief like the face of a foreign national who takes a seat in my office and hears his mother tongue.

Justice

Many people are attracted to certain areas of law, simply out of a sense of wanting to find justice. And we all have our own idea of what this concept of "justice" truly means. Some will seek out work as prosecutors, hoping to punish those they believe to be guilty. Others will go into defense to see to it that the accused receive full protection of their rights.

One thing that both sides will often have in common is an opinion that the system is flawed. Most will agree that no justice is completely blind. Frequently the party who can afford the best lawyer has the best chance of winning.

Regardless, one notices a common theme after a while. The young attorney spends a few years trying cases for the government, whether it is at the state or federal level—then she takes that experience forward and applies its positives in private practice.

But what about justice?

I find myself reminded of the students I knew who concentrated on Environmental Law—thinking that one day they would work in some organization dedicated to preservation— only to take the higher-paying gig with an oil company.

The realities of life are often adjusted by everyday economics. For most of the history of the legal industry, it has been easier to feed a family on what you may earn in the private sector.

However, with shifts in our fiscal state, there are many attorneys doing even better in government careers.

One young man I know, Len, is hoping to get a federal clerkship and then become an Assistant U.S. Attorney. The irony to me is that his first and current position is at a very well known defense firm. I never asked his reasons, but I admire Len's interest in pursuing a career that will ultimately allow him to encounter his definition of justice.

Enthusiasm

Professor Joshua Silverstein of the William H. Bowen School of Law at the University of Arkansas wrote a controversial article that was published in the *University of San Francisco Law Review*, positing that law schools would be wise to do away with the C and increase grade inflation.

The professor opined that inconsistent use of C grades puts students "at an unfair disadvantage when competing for employment with students from institutions that award mostly A's and B's."

He went on to say that without changing current grading systems, "we wouldn't get the psychological benefits of higher grades."

I have one response to this suggestion. And no, it's not the standard "that's coddling students" response I frequently see. In fact, while I neither agree nor disagree with "the fewer C grades" model, I do think it is notable that some of the best law schools have either no grades or odd grading systems, most notably Stanford, Berkeley, University of Chicago, and Yale, all of which consistently are rated among the Top 10 in the U.S.

It reminds me of the old days when some attorneys would talk vociferously about what is deemed "lawyerly"—such as avoiding advertising to attract clients, or claimed payment by credit card to be unprofessional.

These ideas have gone the way of the 8-track tape player.

All I'm saying is that we live in an ever-changing world. While some firms will place great emphasis on one's GPA and alma mater, I think of what makes me pay attention to a law student who applies to intern with my firm.

To me it boils down to one word: enthusiasm.

Have the energy to come up with a unique solution to a problem. Volunteer for an office project. Your dedication will be seen and appreciated. And not only will you make yourself an asset to the firm, but you will probably learn something along the way.

Thrill is gone

"We must all face the choice between what is right and what is easy."

Dumbledore, *Harry Potter and the Goblet of Fire*

There are often stories of how many people succeed financially based on finding their passion and pursuing it. I reference it in other sections of this book. But what about when you've been at the same thing for a very long time and the thrill is gone?

Guess what? Nobody said it was always going to be easy. It goes back to something I learned from my father.

People called my dad "Duke." Ever since I was a young kid, whenever things didn't go my way, Duke would say, "Life's not fair."

And, then, one day, I found myself giving his eulogy, and there I certainly made reference to just how unfair life can be.

But "Life's not fair" is a fine disclaimer to apply to every bummer day, every lost case, and every disappointment of any kind—as long as you remember the other thing that I heard just as often from my father: "Better to have money and be unhappy than to be poor and unhappy."

Wait a second, you say, what if the very thing that makes you so unhappy is also the source of your revenue? Then find a better gig—one that is your passion. But until you do, find a way to make the current situation better.

Perspective will carry you a long way. Hearing or reading inspirational tales often works for me—especially as the years go by. Recently I met a woman from a foreign country, a senior citizen, widowed, and not particularly well off. But she had such a great attitude. She smiled whenever she came into my office.

Working on that lady's case made my day. Every time I saw her, it reaffirmed that I had chosen the right type of career.

It costs so much money to go to law school!

There is an old joke that goes something like this:

Mrs. Green, Mrs. Gold, and Mrs. Silver are old friends who reunite one day after many years.

Not long after ordering their meals, they begin to discuss their children.

Mrs. Green starts: "My son is in medical school, and it's costing me a fortune."

Mrs. Gold responds: "My daughter is in law school, and it's costing me a fortune."

Mrs. Silver turns to both and says, "My son is a plumber. He's making a fortune."

It's a valid point—especially the way things have gone with the economy in the second decade of the 21st century.

But you have to be realistic. Once again, I think of my late father, who said to me when I was still a teenager: "I'm a teacher. One day I will retire. But if you become a lawyer, you can keep working forever, if you want. You just scale down your hours."

Investing in a legal career is a long-term commitment. However, once you have that piece of paper that allows you to practice law, there are just as many options available to you as if you did not have the license. Simply put: the law will always be there for you.

It's your choice what you do with the degree, as you can see, and yes, it's an expensive proposition. I would rather have my Juris Doctor than not have it.

The law will always be an option to those with a license.

So what do you do instead?

Learn from the streetwise. They are—in many ways and very often—smarter than the dumb people like us, with our fancy law degrees.

My dad, the old gym teacher, may have been the world heavyweight champion of street smarts.

On the first occasion that he was diagnosed with cancer, he made it clear that he never wanted anyone to know that he was sick.

I would always wonder how Duke would hide his diagnosis, but somehow, despite all of the chemotherapy, he never lost one hair on his head, and he really never lost much weight either.

He looked pale though. Something about him just appeared to be wrong.

There he was one afternoon, fresh from a session of chemo, when he was in a local pharmacy to pick up some meds.

There he bumped into an old acquaintance, a loudmouth attorney whom he had not seen in years. This jerk took one look at my dad who was—despite his maintenance of hair and weight—not looking his best. The guy said, "Duke, it's been so long, how are you? Boy, you have not gotten any better looking with age."

And how did my old man reply? He could have just said that he was fighting non-Hodgkin's lymphoma, but that was not my father's way.

Instead my dad, without missing a beat, stared at this doofus and gritted his teeth: "And you haven't gotten any smarter with age."

End of the story.

I learned an awful lot from my pop.

For instance, when he showed me how to behave calmly when confronted by an arrogant lawyer, the kind of guy who makes our industry look bad.

The evolution

The world is changing at record speed.

People must learn to adapt. Law schools must evolve too.

I was very fortunate to have an extremely forward-thinking dean when I attended Tulane Law School in the early 1990s. The late John Kramer was a pioneer when it came to approaching how to teach law.

Dean Kramer introduced the first obligatory pro bono requirement in U.S. law schools, which mandated that all students had to do at least twenty hours of voluntary legal work. Kramer also enlarged the law student clinic program, from only three, to eight before he completed his tenure.

His latter accomplishment is proof positive that he was indeed a visionary. Today, clinics are commonplace at all major law schools. Like medical students who must complete their last two years focusing on patient care, I submit that law students too should be working in the field. It only makes sense—you can only get so much out of lecture halls. The real training required to be an attorney should include concentration on helping clients.

Two decades after Dean Kramer grew clinics at Tulane, the clinical program has become far more commonplace at law schools.

Be an artist

"There comes a time when these things start to get in one's way. Expectations can block the light. They can shadow the future, making it more difficult to be free-flowing and creative."

Neil Young, *Waging Heavy Peace*

I've been listening to Neil Young since I was twelve years old, which basically means 30 years of being a fan. I have about 25 of his albums—as well as having seen him four times live. Maybe more than any artist, I relate to him, in the unique approach he's taken throughout his career. I've only come to this realization after a couple of decades working in my own legal practice.

Neil has been playing music for 50 years and expresses frustration about trying to find new ideas. Lawyers can work for 50 weeks and feel exactly the same way. They certainly can feel this way after five years or fifteen years too. Expectations can block out the light, indeed.

The funny part is that I know a few attorneys with 50 years' experience and find that those practitioners tend to seem more "alive" than other folks their age, due to staying active in their work.

And I've written an awful lot during my life, with his music playing in the background.

Neil Young has two sons with varying degrees of cerebral palsy, including one who is quadriplegic and unable to talk. His efforts to make their lives better have been well documented and very inspirational.

Young admitted not long ago that he lived in the U.S. without a green card for several years in the 1960s—a fact I find all too familiar and ironic, as an immigration lawyer.

I have come to realize that art of any form, whether it be music, as it was for me, or photography or painting, can be a powerful inspiration.

Ask yourself. Right now.

Is there an artist who inspires you?

Sometimes a great law student does not make a great lawyer

Many great attorneys started out as law review editors. They pulled all A's and graduated in the top 5 or 10 percent of their class.

However, just as many, if not more, do not make the transition from superior student to outstanding lawyer.

The causes for the shortcomings of these practitioners are numerous:

» an inability to cut it in the real world versus the comparatively sterile classroom

» the lack of "people skills" that are not needed in a research and writing environment but are necessary in a law office

» a lack of interest or experience in business, since there are few law school courses on how to organize a law practice

» the number of law schools that obsess over their graduates' Bar passage rates in lieu of actual job placement

My best training for lawyering was not my legal education, but rather my experience in dealing with the public.

Even well intentioned law professors, who pull their kids out of the classroom and assign them to observe actual trials, can do more to teach the students how to be attorneys.

There's a scene in *Good Will Hunting* in which real-life Harvard dropout Matt Damon's character faces down his antagonist, a fictional Harvard student.

My favorite line in this film comes from the scene: "You dropped a hundred and fifty grand on an education you could've got for a dollar fifty in late charges at the public library."

This point is well made. Books are always there. Making grades based on how well you analyze what you read in them is ultra-important.

But ask yourself, right now, whether you are still in law school or in practice for many years: Can you cut it in the real world?

If you are unsure, this book will help.

Nonpracticing lawyers

I have a group of classmates from law school with whom I keep in varying degrees of contact. Almost all of them do not practice law. Don is in legal publishing, Rich is a court administrator, Stan works in finance, and George has a gig helping folks find jobs. An old law school classmate of mine is now a Congressman.

I heard one say, "The only time I step inside a courtroom is when I get called for jury duty."

Let's face it, you can do anything with a law degree. The knowledge of the legal system will only serve to augment your skills in whatever area you work.

Consider some famous people with law degrees:

World leaders such as Gandhi and Mandela.

American presidents like Taft, Nixon, Ford, Clinton, and Obama.

Some of the greatest baseball managers in history including Branch Rickey, Miller Huggins, and Tony LaRussa.

Iconic sports announcers such as Mel Allen and Howard Cosell went to law school too. Actors even? Yup, you bet. John Cleese. Ozzie Nelson. Raul Julia.

Any chance that these folks' achievements were aided by

their legal studies? You better believe it. Going to law school is like investing in a type of thought process. That mentality can be carried over into many different fields, not just for practicing attorneys.

I communicated recently with Will Shortz, *New York Times* crossword puzzle editor, who has a law degree. He told me:

"While I wanted a career in puzzles, I didn't think that it would be financially possible, so I thought law would be a good way to start. My plan was to practice law for ten years and make enough money to 'retire' and then do what I really wanted. As it turned out, I was able to go into puzzles immediately, as an editor.

Law school is great training for the mind. It teaches you to take a complex issue, separate it into its component parts, and then deal with each one individually—much like solving a puzzle.

Also, law school teaches you a lot about how the wider business world works. As I work for myself and handle all my own contracts, my legal training has been an invaluable help."

Why?

I know folks who graduated law school and ended up teaching high school. Or coaching college sports. Or giving financial advice.

"What happened?" I asked them. How did they end up in roles that do not require law degrees? The responses were interesting to say the least.

For some, it was simply a matter of deciding what they truly loved and going that way.

For others, there was never a dream of commercial litigation or estate planning in their future. They just did not know what they wanted to do after college. Law school seemed to make sense at the time.

Remember: a law degree does not change anything. You can still do whatever you want.

There was one day, a few months after I finished law school, when I spoke to some professors about pursuing a PhD program.

I had pretty much figured that I would practice law but was curious about the academic life too. None of the faculty I met with seemed to feel this plan was a good idea for me, however, as it was obvious to all involved that I wanted to be an attorney.

Now, about twenty years later, I wonder what would have happened if I had gone for the doctorate? No way to know for sure.

The thing is, we all have moments of indecision.

In my heart, I wanted to advocate for people and also make a living, so I knew I made the right choice.

I know other people who have bounced around from job to job. Some practiced, and then switched gears, only to return to the law. Others have held a multitude of gigs with not a second spent in the law.

The one thing I have taken away from all of the discussions I have had with former classmates and colleagues, and even current law students, is that it is very important to question things.

Historically, there has generally been a tendency among some teenagers to question authority. I'd take that a stage further: question everything. After all, at the heart of every good attorney there is that never-ending desire to ask. The Socratic method is based on this philosophy.

There are no wrong answers to most questions. You have to figure out what's right for you.

Wise words from a non-practicing lawyer

This educational, fascinating story comes from Larry Gershberg, a very successful lawyer turned businessman I have known for more than a decade:

"In my first three years of work, I did 10,000 real estate closings (on many days eight closings a day), and after such a short period of time, never met anyone who had done more closings than I did.

Then I moved on to being a Korean bank attorney for about ten years.

On a trip up to Boston, I casually mentioned a business idea to a friend, and that conversation turned into the first all New Balance shoe store. The store opened in a Chicago suburb in 1994.

Over the next several years, there was a Korean banking crisis where many banks went out of business or were consumed by other banks, and we lost our client base. In 1998 I decided to open New Balance North Jersey, while continuing to practice law.

Law became more stressful. I started going to sleep at night wondering if there was something I had forgotten to do that day and got terrible anxiety.

As we opened the first New Balance concept store, the company went to other top shoe dealers around the country and opened more concept stores. At the first national meeting of the concept storeowners, I looked around the room and thought, 'Eleven shoe store owners and one business lawyer; this should be easy.' The chain now has 170 stores throughout North America, and for ten years in a row, our North Jersey store has been number one in the country. I consider my years as a business attorney to be incredibly valuable to our store's success.

Our motto of customer service being the most important thing, and our trademark of 'just return it,' have worked, making customers happy one at a time.

We have now expanded and opened New Balance Westchester, and recently added New Balance Princeton.

I retired from law, sell shoes, and live happily ever after."

Mentorship is investing in the legal profession

Some things in life are inevitable. If your name is Dennis and you're a fighter, chances are certain people are going to nickname you "the Menace."

How about the folks who developed Post-it notes? Despite it taking the better part of a decade, that product had to break through at some point.

I am not a superstitious person, but I do believe in fate. Destiny is a big part of how things evolve in life and also in the law.

Sometimes, though, you have to make your own destiny.

So what if you're sitting there reading this, trying to find the magic answers to key questions like "How can I improve as an attorney?" or "What should I do once I graduate law school?"

…And what if you're stumped?

One potential solution that will never hurt is to locate successful people—not just lawyers. Observe their way of doing things, and then try to emulate them.

Early on in my career, I appeared many times before several judges who were very experienced, both on the bench and as litigators beforehand. They actually took it upon themselves to mentor new attorneys.

It was not unusual for them to steer hearings in a certain direction. They did this impartially. It did not matter if one (or both) of the lawyers in the hearings was a novice. These judges, I believe, wished to teach hard-working practitioners how to try cases in real life.

They also wanted to keep their calendars moving and ultimately ensure that the litigants received competent representation. Frequently the judges would grumble that so many unprepared lawyers were appearing before them. They would be willing to help out a young attorney for obvious reasons, but not be so open-minded about older folks who—in their opinion—had no excuse for their lack of planning for trial.

It made court less intimidating for lawyers, not to mention the actual parties whose lives could be affected so significantly by the outcome of the proceedings.

The mentorship extended outside the courtroom. One great judge, the late William Strasser, invited me to speak at a seminar he was moderating, when I was barely out of my twenties. He knew that I had been handling many cases involving a very nuanced area, and that I was capable of explaining the law. That event led to me presenting lectures dozens of times since then.

The lesson? Find your mentor or—better still—be one. I try to be the same mentor to my law interns as this judge was to me.

Specialize

An older lawyer, Pete, started complaining to me. "Nothing is the way it's supposed to be anymore. People used to come to us, spend five or ten minutes evaluating our credentials, then a half hour discussing their problems. They would finish up by talking fees. They were satisfied with your qualifications and rates, and then they would pay you. You would put some papers in the folder, eventually read them, write something, send it out, and wait for them to get what they wanted, which was usually more money."

I shook my head, feeling sad for this man..

"You mean it was really that easy?" I asked, although I did not subscribe to his approach.

"Yup." Pete shrugged and scratched off a lottery ticket with a dirty penny, one of many in a pile of crumpled cards and grey shavings.

Personally, I do not believe it was ever that easy. I spent more time on everything from the beginning.

I'm not saying I'm the greatest lawyer in the world, but I believe in being very careful. Every detail counts.

Here's how I did it then. Here's how I do it now. Someone comes in with a problem. Often they've been to multiple attorneys who were stymied by their case. These lawyers told them it was too tough or impossible to fix.

I say, "Let me have a look." And I sit there. And analyze. And yes, sometimes I do not find an answer. In that case, I tell the client to save his money. My honesty helps me sleep at night, and it also keeps my reputation strong.

But often I do find a solution. Maybe not an iron-clad, 100 percent lock, but certainly enough to take a pretty reasonable chance. And I win a lot. Why? Because I'm not a jack-of-all-trades. I'm not a hack. I am not what is referred to as a "briefcase schlepper."

In the law today, specializing is crucial. Recently I began to read about areas that I had never heard of. For example, many commercial litigators tout themselves as "Bet the company" litigation experts. In my own field, I know enough obscure law to surpass 90 percent or more of my peers simply due to many years of experience concentrated in very specific areas.

One white-collar defense lawyer, John, tells me, "General practice can be malpractice."

I agree. After all, would you go to the same doctor for a broken clavicle as you would for a scratched cornea? I certainly wouldn't. But in law, all you need is a license, and you can decide to start taking fees for most any case. Divorce. Estate planning. Accidents. Bankruptcy. Real estate. Personally, I would refer people to five different attorneys for the above issues.

Not everyone feels that way, of course. It's no wonder that most lawyers have to deal with the public image of being shysters.

I once heard a martial arts expression attributed to Renzo Gracie: "If you want to teach them nothing, show them everything."

This is a fairly straightforward philosophy, but so rarely followed in life.

I am not faulting people for trying to earn, but come on—you can't try to know everything. You are doing your client and yourself a disservice. Better to be great at one thing than mediocre, or flat out lousy, at a whole bunch of stuff.

Special needs

In my field, I have gained a bit of a reputation for assisting families whose children have special needs. It happened organically. I helped one woman, a single mother facing deportation, whose daughter suffered from seizures. Next thing I knew, she told a friend whose child was profoundly disabled. Thus I had another such case. Word of mouth spread.

Over the years I have found some of my rewarding work in helping immigrants whose U.S. citizen children have been afflicted with a variety of medical conditions, ranging from attention deficit to physical challenges.

This experience has made me consider an area of law that is deeply in need of more lawyers: education law.

A quick search on special education lawyers in New York on a high-traffic law directory yielded only half a dozen firms listed in the state. Although there are certainly more education attorneys than those named on the website, there is clearly a critical shortage.

Advocacy for parents needing help fighting with school districts is extremely important work. Yet very few attorneys take on this mission. That's no surprise when very few law schools even offer coursework in the field.

I reviewed a well-regarded resource on education law and located only thirteen law schools that offer children's advocacy programs.

The stress of this work may be as tough as in any legal specialty, but the gifts are immeasurable. Consider strong representation for a kid with a disability. That is a wonderful way to use a law degree.

I once had a t-shirt from a charity event years ago that proclaimed:

"The toughest people... are those who speak for those who cannot speak."

That t-shirt tells us a great deal about the devotion of attorneys in the special education field. Taking on school districts—which often retain large firms to back up their plans to lowball students out of receiving better services—is tough work.

But the payback is enormous. You can forever change a child's life by convincing an administrative judge to grant the requested educational plan, despite the school's gripes that it may be costly. How can one place a price tag on saving a kid from a future that is bleak, if that kid does not get the proper academic support as early as possible?

Styles make fights

I never noticed any discrimination on the job until I began working with female litigators, who would zealously defend our clients, only to face staunch opposition from male lawyers.

If I fought that hard, that would be expected. But for some men who are threatened by women, this aggression presents a problem.

Now, I have no hassle with folks who fight back. But if they are doing so simply for gender reasons, then that's wrong.

It is not just rival attorneys, either. A lawyer's gender, said jury and trial consultant Paul H. Jepsen more than a decade ago, was relevant to jurors who evaluate women litigators more on their appearance and dress than their male peers.

However, this syndrome can work to a female's favor when the judge or attorney across the aisle is a woman too. I have seen women judges who faced much worse bias in their early careers take younger lawyers of the same gender under their wing, mentor them, and even acknowledge how they understand the extra pressures.

My colleague Laura Gasiorowski—whom I mentioned previously—did death penalty work until the birth of the first of her three children. She practices part-time now while raising them.

She told me a very compelling story about her career.

As a law student intern, she assisted on a capital case that changed her life. The client was charged with killing his girlfriend's infant within days of his release after serving time for burglary. The baby was found in his crib, shaken to death. The autopsy report was just horrifying.

Laura was not really a pro-defendant kind of person back then—she would have preferred the prosecutor's office. As such, she was convinced the guy was guilty.

Halfway through trial, her boss sent her to enlarge a piece of paper and have it made into a poster board for the jury to see. It was a letter from the girlfriend to her client, in jail, which the warden had never delivered, and which the prosecution had held back in discovery.

Highlighted were the words "I am sorry I kilt the baby but I did it for us."

The district attorney dropped the case that day.

Laura says now, "The thought that I believed in his guilt, just based on the indictment and evidence I saw, and that the jury would likely have believed in his guilt as well, and sentenced an innocent man to death, freaked me out. So did the idea, one with some basis in fact, that the prosecutor may have known all along that the person he indicted and took to trial in a capital case was not responsible for that baby's terrible death. Honestly, it was an epiphany. From that day on, I had found my calling. I worked with some other lawyers who did death penalty work, and that became the catalyst for becoming a criminal defense attorney."

I also asked Laura about being a woman in the legal field. She had a lot to say: "When I was younger, I had to listen to the sexual exploits of my boss and co-workers and attend an office Christmas party at a strip joint.

The partner of a prominent firm interviewed me and asked if I wanted a drink while he pulled my chair over to his side of the desk.

I have had judges yell at me, while I made appearances in criminal court, that my boss better not send one of his secretaries again, or had others inquire whether I was even a lawyer.

A co-worker who often handled traffic court sent me in his stead one day, instructing me that a municipal prosecutor would be more likely to dismiss my client's traffic violations if I showed some cleavage.

Frankly, I think that I have been harassed on more than one occasion, whether by a client or an employer or a co-worker, but I just soldiered on, and as I got older, I got smarter with regard to whom I chose to work for, and how I handled the negative interactions with peers and clients.

I know that I am a good lawyer and have some real talents and skills, and that confidence is not only armor but also a repellant for boorish behavior. On balance, the idiots have been in the minority.

The reality is that I have had some amazing male mentors, people who respected me and helped me in my career, and they have always been very sensitive to the difficulties I sometimes faced as a young female lawyer. Now I never think about it at all, and I have no interest in defining myself as a woman lawyer."

A trial is often a fight, and it is frequently said in the combat sports arena that styles make fights. I have often advised the women who work with me to know their opponent's styles. If they expect a battle from a perceived sexist, be ready for it. Present the opposing side's worst questions on direct examination to disarm them. By the time the cross exam comes, there may be little left to cover.

There is a great old calypso song that goes like this:

"I say that the women today

Are smarter than the men in every way

That's right, the women are smarter."

To me there is no doubt about it. The women are smarter. And that's why they still face so much discrimination, even in the 21st century.

I feel if I am happy, I am successful.
Gaby Ponce, *World's Greatest Female Vert Skateboarder*

"I hate being a lawyer."

This one is tough. But consider the fact that many people, not just lawyers, do not enjoy their work. You may have to walk away at some point if you are truly miserable.

For me the easiest advice to combat the unhappy feeling that comes for some attorneys is to rededicate yourself to the job. I am hardcore. I monitor my emails, phone calls, and letters 24/7 via laptop, cell phone, and the mailbox.

To me, it's simple. Every call is a lead. Every lead is a case.

And my daughter loves to skateboard.

Caught you, didn't I?

"What does this have to do with being a lawyer?" you ask.

Well, there's a professional skateboarder, Gaby Ponce, who has won Gold at X Games.

My daughter skated with her a couple of times before Gaby moved out West.

Gaby told me that she practices five to six days a week, but that most of all, for her, skateboarding is fun—and if she is having fun and is happy, then she is successful.

I think every *person*, far less every lawyer, can learn something from Gaby Ponce.

Realize that you have to be committed to be successful.

If your commitment cannot defeat your dissatisfaction with the law, then consider the non-practicing lawyer route. You can always go back to the law in the future.

An old classmate of mine, Liz, has two Ivy League diplomas, and has had about half a dozen great jobs. She was amazed when she discovered that I have sat in the same building doing the same job ever since I started my career.

Maybe I am lucky. I don't know for sure. I just knew that I was never going to be point guard for the Knicks.

Perhaps it's a matter of changing your specialty and finding a way to do what you really love every day.

Thinner herd

In early 2013 *The New York Times* reported that there were 30,000 applicants to law schools for the upcoming year. This number represented a 20 percent decrease from 2011 and a 38 percent decrease from 2010. Notably, there were 100,000 applicants to law schools in 2004, and the *Times* expected about half of that figure a decade later.

The newspaper went on to analyze data and give all the expected quotations from professors and experts, but I can explain it in one sentence: Law school is expensive, and there are not enough jobs at the moment.

So what to do, what to do? If you are contemplating law school, it's a damn good question. I personally think there are enough generally frustrated attorneys out there that more new lawyers would only worsen things for them.

If you have a good attitude, though, this lesser applicant pool should motivate you to jump into a thinning herd and expect to make a successful career three years after you start school.

I would not start looking for alternatives to law, if I knew in my guts that I wanted to be an attorney. The whole thing reminds me of a sad but true story of a retiring judge who once told me many years ago that he was fed up with unprepared attorneys. I replied that I felt sorry for their clients but did not need the competition.

I think of Vince Lombardi:

"Unless a man believes in himself and makes a total commitment to his career and puts everything he has into it—his mind, his body, his heart—what's life worth to him?"

In my mind, if you tell a law student or lawyer that things are tough, the reply should be, "Duh. When has it ever been easy to do it right?"

The flipside of fear is success

My late grandfather Louie was a wonderful man. Everyone who knew him loved him. As a young man, he had to quit college after one semester to go to work. He ended up managing men's clothing stores for more than 40 years, and he was good at it.

Nevertheless, there were limits to what he could accomplish as a retail manager.

If things had been different back then, I'm quite certain that Louie would have gotten his degree and could have been an outstanding attorney with his gift of gab, incredible memory, and personality.

But one other thing I remember about him was how his fears continually stopped him. Louie never pursued business opportunities that came his way. He never bought into offers, due to being afraid he would lose everything.

I learned a lot from hearing about his experiences, but the most important lesson I can share is this: the opposite of being afraid is the very distinct probability that if you work hard enough on a new venture, you will succeed.

The phrase "the greater the risk, the greater the reward" is often heard in the context of the stock market. But it applies to just about every business venture, including a career as a lawyer. Taking the risk is to surmount fear. To surmount fear is to succeed.

Train ride

The first year law grads bump into each other on the train home to Brooklyn. They are all tired and sweaty from a long day in July in New York but someone decides to compare notes.

"What're you doing?"

"Working at a Terrible Law Firm. I hate it."

"How 'bout you?"

"Yeah, I'm at a Boring Bureaucracy. It's miserable."

"And you?"

A long pause.

One of my associates, Maggie, had to speak. She felt guilty because she actually enjoyed her career. Reluctantly she admitted this fact to the others.

One congratulated her on finding a satisfying place to practice law.

One kept his mouth shut.

Maggie related this story to me not long after. I told her not to feel guilty that she chose a path that is rewarding. She planned carefully with clerking and internships that helped her stand out from the pack when I was looking for a new associate. She deserves to feel proud of her achievements.

I looked around in law school and played the game of process of elimination. Every time I took a class I did not enjoy, I made a mental note not to pursue that area of law. By the time I graduated, I was pretty certain about what I wanted to do. In my case it was immigration; I know others who felt the same about matrimonial, estate planning, and bankruptcy law. Fast forward all these years later, and I know I made the right choice.

Hypothetically let's just say that I had made a mistake.

You can always hit the reset button.

It is never too late to change careers or firms, or switch from private to public sector, or vice versa, even in a tough economy. You just have to have guts and want it bad enough. Those two go hand in hand.

Fear is a powerful motivator. But you know what? The opposite of fear is courage, and that force makes the best lawyers I know. They may fear losing a case or a particular judge but they get out there and try their best every day. Those folks end up winning the most—no shortcuts.

So if you hate what you do, think about your options, do careful research, and take a chance at doing something different with your degree, your license, and your experience. You just might end up liking your new gig.

THE SECOND DEGREE

Running the Best Practice You Can

———

What is effective management?

About fifteen years ago, my friend Jack worked at a midsized Northeastern law firm. Every December, it was time for bonuses. I was shocked to discover that this office had a policy in which only 20 percent of the attorneys received a little extra in their paycheck. Apparently this was performance-based.

When I look back at this procedure, I am even more appalled today than I was then. Today I have a family to support. My objection to the "only one out of every five gets a bonus" rule has to do with my feelings about the holidays. The partners in charge of the bonuses should have taken the season into consideration. The overall morale in the office in January, and likely after, had to be terrible for the other 80 percent. Why not give everyone a bonus and adjust salaries?

The Christmas bonus story is a microcosm of every bad decision that management makes. I don't care if you supervise a staff of two, two hundred, or two thousand. You have to treat your employees with the same patience and understanding that you give to the clients. To wit: we have all known lawyers who yell at both their staff and clients. Some of these folks take this terrible personality trait into every facet of their lives. From time to time, I have dealt with colleagues who were unjustifiably rude to me.

Example: I once called a fellow, Roy, with an office in a particular area. I asked him how the price of real estate was in his region. He abruptly grumbled, "I am not a broker," and hung up the phone.

I would like to give Roy the benefit of the doubt. Maybe he was having a bad day. Maybe his wife was sick. Still, I could never understand why it was so difficult for him to just be nice.

What I learned from phys ed teachers

My dad, Duke, was a baseball coach and gym teacher in the 1960s and 70s. As he got older, he and my mom opened their little greeting card shop. Every day after he finished work at the high school he drove to the card store and put in a whole other shift. Essentially, he worked two jobs for many years.

Some of the others in the Phys Ed Department, branded "dumb jocks" by a few of their peers decades ago, were equally motivated to find sources of extra income. One gym teacher, Saul, got a degree in chiropractic medicine and then began a second career in that field. Another phys ed instructor, Kevin, got a black belt in karate and opened his own school on nights and weekends. Another lifeguarded and parlayed that into a job as a director at a pool club.

Meanwhile, many of the classroom teachers hung out in the building after their days ended. They sat around and shared glib remarks with one another, mainly about politics and the arts. Duke would point out that there was nothing wrong with this choice. He was friendly with the people who hung around after the last bell rang, but he was too busy to sit still.

The well read, articulate educators were often the ones sitting and chatting, while the folks best known for blowing whistles and making kids run laps did not stop to gab. They were too busy pursuing other careers.

I often thought of this when I left a courthouse and ran back to my office to see clients. There are always going to be the attorneys who go get coffee with colleagues and talk about how this law should be changed or that policy stinks. I have no problem with these people. If it makes them happy to sit on self-appointed ad hoc java bean committees, more power to them.

But for me, it's more important to maximize my time. I would rather serve on a formal board, such as when I chaired a section of my state bar association in my limited free time.

I prefer to use every minute of my time pursuing legitimate angles on how to grow a client base, no matter how many years I am in practice.

The sad truth

I do see a trend among unhappy lawyers, especially when no money comes in.

What do they do?

Do they kick themselves in the butt? No.

1. They get more discouraged.

2. They lose their energy.

3. They stop returning phone calls.

4. They fail to read important legal documents.

Their failure and misery is a self-fulfilling prophecy.

Time and time again, in good economies or bad, the worst sin an attorney can commit, short of actual crime, is to be negligent. You can be the most gifted orator in your jurisdiction but your skills are useless if you miss deadlines. It happens every day.

Apathy will kill a lawyer faster than anything.

Ineffective assistance

I frequently have had to work on cases in which a motion was filed due to prior counsel prejudicing my client as a result of ineffective assistance.

The one that stands out most in my mind dates back to the 90s. A lawyer almost got his client deported due to a deficiently filed appeal. I made a last-minute petition to the court and got the matter reopened, ultimately resulting in my client receiving a green card.

Why do I remember this case so vividly? The excuse the first lawyer gave for his mistake.

This guy actually wrote that he was negligent due to taking on too many cases and not having enough time to handle them all. I would say that you couldn't make this excuse up, but he went with it.

Nobody's perfect, but this mistake was egregious. The attorney was ultimately suspended from practicing law, which was very sad—what would have been even sadder was if my client had been removed from the United States due to his errors.

I pity the lawyer for his incompetence. However, I felt sympathy for the anxiety that he had caused my client, faced with being banished from America because this fellow could not do his job properly. Luckily it all worked out for my client.

It would be one thing if he was the only one, but the tragedy is that I have seen this type of pattern, and not infrequently. Lawyers take on work. The same old theme ensues. It is easy to collect the retainer; the tough part is getting the work done.

Efficiency and organization are central to running a good practice. This advice may sound like common sense, but in real life I have seen so many lawyers suffer from the disease of "solo practitioner-itis." This condition is characterized by not hiring enough good help, trying to do too much at once, and following it up by not doing anything at all.

I have always surrounded myself with talented people. Warren Buffet once said:

"It's better to hang out with people better than you. Pick out associates whose behavior is better than yours, and you'll drift in that direction."

This is not a sprint. It's a cross-country race.

One of the biggest mistakes attorneys make is improperly measuring the bottom line. They calculate success and failure in the short run (e.g. "we had a lousy year" or "this was a great month").

I am all for being realistic about how business is trending, but I also feel that—at least for those of us in private practice—there has to be a long-term plan. If things aren't going to your satisfaction at any one moment, do something about it. Never accept failure.

I look at other firms' errors and try to learn from them.

Some try to get too big, only to collapse after a century of leadership in the legal field. We can all probably think of at least one such example; I knew some brilliant lawyers at those houses.

From the demises of those firms, I learned that many attorneys should keep their work small enough to control.

Another similar example is the multi-state firm, nowhere near the size of the aforementioned ones. These outfits might employ dozens, as opposed to hundreds, of attorneys. But as Earl—a former partner in such an entity—once told me, "We were too busy practicing law to run offices in five cities."

I can only shake my head at that comment. I just cannot believe that a group of educated people did not think things through carefully enough to realize that a managing partner, thoughtfully selected, is essential to make such an operation work.

The practice of law is like cross-country running. You deal with obstacles and the elements, climb mountains, and sometimes go flying downhill at breakneck speed. A great runner can win a cross-country race.

Sprinting in the law is never advisable, though. That type of pace will kill you over the long haul.

Anger management

Anger is a powerful force when channeled properly. It emboldens some attorneys and fuels their drive. Managed appropriately, an angry lawyer can win cases.

But the reality is that I have seen anger hurt most people in the legal profession. Their minds become clouded, and they behave irrationally.

I never will forget one time when I was standing in a hallway outside a courtroom. A lawyer, Felix, was furious with his client. I have no idea what the man did to upset the attorney. All I recall is Felix raising his voice in public, and saying, "Don't talk to me like that; I'm your lawyer—you treat me with respect, or I will give you your money back right now!"

Seeing how that looks on the page makes it seem comical.

Now, I have no idea what the root of the conflict was, but the last thing I would ever tell a client who has upset me is that I was going to give him a refund after all the work has been done.

I will admit to losing my patience with clients once in a while, particularly when I was younger. Today, though, I remind myself that most folks who seek legal advice do so for a reason.

Our job as attorneys is to solve problems, and often to fix lives. To lose one's control, to become angry, is no way to behave professionally.

No case is too small

As a kid I loved reading *Encyclopedia Brown* books. He was the juvenile detective who solved crimes for his dad, the police chief, as well as his own preteen friends and neighbors. His motto was, "No case too small."

This slogan stands out in my mind—particularly when I get called in on something that another attorney might find too petty. There is no case too small. Every client's problem is the most important to him. If you do a solid job fixing it, that client will be more than happy to impress your success upon his friends and family.

Ego is the lawyer's worst enemy when it comes time to decide whether to accept certain tasks. I have no problem taking on what we refer to as "vanilla" cases. In fact, there are days when those issues are welcome, especially when we are buried in emergencies.

I have a client who once sang in several world-famous rock groups. He played Madison Square Garden and was frequently on MTV in the 1980s. Three decades later he still works center stage in the music industry and can still sell plenty of tickets in certain parts of the world. But what I find most significant about his long career is his lack of ego.

Even in his heyday, he never turned down smaller gigs. He did backing vocals on many artists' albums. He acted in bit parts in films too. Why? Because they were paying him.

I notice a similar pattern in the career of Brooke Shields. The parts she takes can be in kids' films, TV shows, or on Broadway; she has worked consistently from childhood into her late forties.

My rock star client and Ms. Shields taught me that a payday is as important as continuing to do what they both love to do: perform.

As attorneys we have to think the same way. Get consistent work doing what you enjoy. Some cases may not be as exciting as others, but put your all into every one of them. No case too small.

Million Dollar Arms

Ever hear of Million Dollar Arm? Yeah, I hadn't either...

Well, it was started as a reality show in India and was released as a movie in American cinemas in May 2014. The show featured a search for pitchers, with the winner throwing the fastest and most accurate baseball.

With nearly 40,000 contestants on the show, the champion, a fellow named Singh, and the runner-up, Patel, not only gained notoriety and prizes, but went to the U.S., where they both signed with the Pittsburgh Pirates.

Yes, that would be the same Pirates who had 20 consecutive losing seasons.

What we learn from this story is that if you hate losing but don't want to give up, you start to look for unique solutions. If my law firm didn't enjoy success, I might search for talent in much the same manner.

So, the Pirates signed the first two Indians ever to major league baseball contracts.

Singh and Patel pitched first in 2009 for the Pirates' Gulf Coast League affiliate. The team consisted of nine Dominicans, nine Venezuelans, six Americans, two Puerto Ricans, a Colombian, a Mexican, a Panamanian, an Australian, a Canadian, and a South African.

I am reminded of some of the best Grateful Dead lyrics:

"Once in a while you get shown the light

In the strangest of places if you look at it right."

Are the Pirates any better because they signed these experimental projects? Not necessarily, but you have to give them credit for trying to come up with novel ideas.

Days between

There are days in the law that, quite frankly, stink. Occasionally it seems that all the clients are unhappy with how their case is going, and why are they having to pay these bills, and why hasn't the judge issued a ruling, and how come the law says this or that.

It is at these precise moments that I recall something I was often told by the ultimate pragmatist, my dad: "All people are neither happy nor sad."

Sure, you get the truly depressed and, equally, the folks who are always whistling a tune, but on balance, everyone has good days and bad days.

And it appears to be that we all have our bad days as attorneys.

It is usually days when you worry about paying the bills, the days where a motion gets denied— the days when everything is wrong.

But these days pass.

When I am having one of those bad days, I enjoy thinking about the greatest successes of my career.

Those are the best days, and the thought of those best days helps the bad ones pass.

On the tour bus and the passion

Once I spent some time with guitar icon Zakk Wylde. He invited my family and me to hang out on his tour bus.

So there we were, a relatively normal American husband and wife, with our then-seven-year-old daughter and four-year-old son. And a giant man-child with the requisite long hair of a heavy metal axeman, not to mention a pair of matching braids hanging from his chin.

We chatted for hours about everything from music to sports to parenthood to how we supported our families.

It was clear that Zakk knew as much about being an attorney

as I knew about ripping guitar solos in front of stadium-sized audiences.

His oft-repeated preface to sentences to my wife went, "When your man gets home from doing his lawsuits…"

I was charmed and amused. All Zakk knew about lawyers was that he had some of them on retainer when someone needed to get sued for things like copyright infringement.

Similarly, although I am a huge music fan, I cannot play a note to save my life.

I'm referring specifically to his passion. He did not talk about the excitement of rock stardom, not even for a second. What he did mention was how long he'd practiced his passion before he made it. I could relate to his devotion to his craft. I have brought that attitude to my endeavors at law with just as much commitment.

In fact, the man was so egoless that if you did not know he played with Ozzy Osbourne and Black Label Society for twenty years, you would assume he was a gas station attendant in Jackson, New Jersey—which he happened to be, before he made it.

I took a lot away from that day. This guy had every right to be a pompous ass—or at least many people in entertainment feel that way. But he was the most normal guy you could ever meet. I could not help but think of all of the attorneys I've known with overblown egos. Yet here's this guy with 1.4 million Facebook fans who is talking to me about everyone from Django Reinhardt to Mike Piazza—but not about himself.

I get back to work a couple of days later and find myself in a courthouse surrounded by folks in my field, a few of whom had no trouble at all displaying their incredibly high opinions of themselves.

Gives you some food for thought.

The telecommute

The rate of telecommuting by attorneys has risen, as it has in most industries. Smart phones, teleconferencing, and databases with firm files in the cloud facilitate work from home or anywhere.

Seriously, if I could work from home more often, I would do it. The savings of time, money, and fuel, and the ecological efficiency all make this method attractive.

When I was a kid, my old man always used to advise me to get an office that did not require me to rely on bridges or tunnels. He was 110 percent right on that. But I would add more to his point. Why depend on mass transit or your car if you can get a brief written without traveling to an office?

Twenty-some odd years ago I clerked for a judge who was amazed when I told him that law students could avoid libraries altogether by using the relatively infant Westlaw and Lexis.

Nowadays it's a no-brainer to do work remotely. It's more efficient too, not just to save time on the road or rails. With a cell, laptop, and tablet, you can accomplish so much. Reply immediately via phone or email to clients and colleagues. Research and write all you need in your sweats. Heck, with telephonic hearings becoming more common, even court appearances can be done from the comforts of home.

Now I am not suggesting for one second that telecommuting will be the perfect solution for many. Face-to-face client meetings are a need for millions of lawyers globally. Judges still need to see litigants in person, too. But an increase in technology can certainly solve some problems and keep people happy and productive.

And isn't that what this book is all about?

Wall plaques

I've just read an interesting series of internet exchanges between veteran attorneys online, nationwide. The topic was the significance of plaques for the office wall, commemorating years in the profession and the like.

Opinions varied from "I put them up to impress clients" to "I think it is egotistical."

My conclusion is the following:

If an athlete wins a championship trophy, does he display it?

If a scientist is awarded a prize for important research, does she announce it?

Lawyers need to let potential and current clients know about their accolades.

The reasons are many.

1. First impressions are extraordinarily valuable, both on the website and on the wall.

2. Being shy is not best in a field in which effective communication results in victory.

3. Accomplishments resulting in notability must be publicized to grow a client base.

4. If you made *Law Review*, would you not emphasize it on your résumé?

Achievements are to be lauded; one would never think twice of promoting an Olympic medal on a Wheaties box, so why would a lawyer fail to hang up wall plaques?

"It's an honor to meet you"

The other day a new client came in. He started by telling me that he had watched all of the video lectures I have available online. Then he commented, "It's an honor to meet you."

I replied, "It's a pleasure to have you in my office."

We spoke at length about the many lawyers who could not assist him, and how he even observed that the majority lacked interest in his case.

He hired me that day, largely due to his belief that I understood how to resolve his issues, and also because of my genuine enthusiasm.

I thought about our exchange for quite some time later in the afternoon. The gentleman had spoken to me like I would talk to a hero from my youth, someone I idolized as a third-grader, like Johnny Bench or one of the guys in KISS.

But his words went beyond that.

There is a clear distinction between fan worship by a seven-year-old and the admiration expressed by an adult who has spent countless hours searching for an attorney to solve his legal dilemma.

I realized then the same thing that I have often thought about the power of the internet. For no money at all, I can share valuable information with the whole world. Anyone out there can call or email me and I will answer their questions.

Often these folks become the best clients, and not only do you rescue them from a major problem, but they go on to laud your work publicly. We both benefit.

Loyalty and law

This concept stands alone as to what makes a great legal team. The clichéd, cutthroat divisions that occur all too frequently in many law firms have caused the downfall of so many great attorneys.

When the people can stand together, they all win. When you know your peers have your back, it's worth a million dollars.

It goes beyond money. A wonderful thing it truly is, to know that when a lawyer is challenged, others will rise up with him to defeat obstacles, whether we are talking about adversaries, difficult legal issues, or hard-to-please clientele.

The loyalty should extend to support staff as well.

I had a secretary for several years who stayed with me until she relocated. I do not hear from her very often, but when I do, she always mentions how she never had a boss—before or since—who would stick up for her when disgruntled phone callers (or anyone else) hassled her. Maybe it's my paternal instinct, but I would never allow mistreatment of a colleague.

Devotion to your team will pay off in countless ways. A strong legal entity gains ground quickly. Word gets out fast about a group of lawyers who work as one.

Of course, that loyalty should always be extended to clients. They will love you for your commitment to them, and so will their family members and friends.

As I sit here writing this passage, I think of a man whom my team defended over the course of more than five years. The final victory occurred mere weeks ago.

Today I fielded a call from the fellow's cousin, who lives nearly 100 miles away from my office. Sure enough, my client's relative has made an appointment to meet with me.

Whom do I have to thank for this referral? My team.

If I consider myself successful as an attorney, then it was due to my mother who is illiterate; she was never able to educate herself for various reasons (political, gender, income, etc.). Her greatest upset was that she never had the opportunity to educate herself. She always emphasized how important education is and how fortunate I was to have the opportunity to do so. She always inspired me to be best that I could be.

Melinda Basaran, *Attorney*

Singular dedication

My law firm website has a three-word message: "Dedication. Success. Freedom."

The idea was to convey our mission to the public: We are dedicated. That dedication leads to success. Consequently, our clients will experience a feeling of freedom. Freedom from worry about their problems, freedom to live in this country peacefully, freedom to work and travel.

But it all starts with dedication. I think about work all of the time. Sure, I have time off to spend with family and interests outside of the office.

Still, my clients and their cases are always on my mind. The dedication runs deep. I really hate to lose. Losing, to paraphrase Vince Lombardi, can become a habit.

So I commit myself to winning. It's not an ego thing—it just makes sense. Winning cases means I've done my job the best way I know how. It means that I've taken my career seriously. It saves people's lives. There is no better feeling than helping them.

A dedicated attorney does right by his family. He feeds his kids. He pays the bills. Then, he goes outside the core of his existence and begins to create livelihoods for others who work with him. I love the idea that I have given deserving attorneys and law students a place to learn and earn.

Some of the folks on my team have families to feed too, and I feel a responsibility for all of this. So I stay focused on work. My dedication is to my clients and my fellow lawyers.

Wizarding world

My wife and I have taken our kids to the *Harry Potter* theme park twice. As an attorney who always seeks out new ways to find clients in need, I am amazed by the unique marketing spectacle of the Wizarding World.

There is something truly awe-inspiring about this Universal Studios venue, not just the feeling that you've stepped into a *Harry Potter* film. It's the energy.

Recently a Broadway star was in my office and stated, "I really like the energy in here." That's how I feel when I'm at Potter World. Folks from all over the planet converge on Orlando to wait two hours to taste their first sip of Butterbeer... at ten bucks a cup, I might add.

Even the gift shops have two-hour lines! The whole experience is fascinating. The whole time we enjoy the park, there's a part of me making mental notes on how the creators must have planned it. I pay attention to every detail, how perfectly they've replicated streets and castles from the eight *Harry Potter* movies.

What does this teach me about how I practice law, though?

For my money, the Potter Park is the best one in America— better than Disney or a New Jersey boardwalk beset with ancient amusement rides.

Why? Because it just feels... real.

And that reality—based on a series of fantasy books and cinema—is so incredible. There are folks from New York,

Idaho, South Africa, Japan, and the UK all excitedly taking it all in, regardless of age.

Clients often tell me, "You really understand my problem, and I think you can help me."

My response: "I cannot promise a successful outcome, but my team and I will do our best."

The people who put the Wizarding World of Harry Potter on an empty lot in Florida did their best, and it's working. People are saying things like, "I want to live here." The many billions of dollars that J.K. Rowling's ideas have generated inspire me to give my clients an experience that is just as satisfying.

After all, a great attorney is often also a magician. But to master wizardry, there must be hard work, practice, training, and then, victory.

That's as real as it gets.

THE THIRD DEGREE

Being the Best Lawyer You Can Be

In 2005, my father died after battling cancer four different times between ages 50 and 63. The thing I recall most about his various treatments was the service he received.

I always thought it was nice of his oncologist to personally call him with test results on the same day. The doctor would call our house, sometimes at 10:00 pm. He obviously did not want my dad to have to wait for news. I am sure he did the same with his other patients— it's called "caring."

This is a book about how to practice law a new way. "New" does not mean "wimpy"—quite the opposite. You can be stronger than ever before by taking a greater interest in your clients' lives.

An older lawyer, Terrence, once told me that you shouldn't let the clients "waste your time" by listening to their problems, unless, of course, those problems have to do directly with their case.

I disagree with this opinion.

I grew up in the family retail business. I listened to regular customers' problems for an hour at a time, only to have them finally drop eighty-five cents on the counter for the greeting cards they purchased. They could have gone to any store to buy their cards, but I listened to their problems. So they came back for every holiday, every friend's birthday, every time they fell in love and needed a card for a new paramour.

Listening brings people back—especially when you really care about them. Is it any great surprise that the best clients are the ones who return for every legal service, and better still, bring family and friends?

Respond

Long before most attorneys had begun to study how to cope with the changes in our economy, I began working with the notion that all clients, big and small, really want one thing: immediate response.

While this may seem like a simple solution, the fact is that most attorneys believe that they are too busy to answer calls and emails quickly. This is not true. It is simply a matter of putting the client communications before more frivolous matters.

I have always worked with the 24-hour rule. By this I mean, if the client calls or emails, do your best to reply within 24 hours or less. This includes weekends and holidays. Yes, I'm serious. See more below.

Of course, developments in technology have made it much

easier to accomplish this task. Between my cell, tablet, laptop, and desktop, I have no trouble staying on top of all messages. It takes no time at all to answer questions.

What is far more time-consuming is procrastinating with the belief that you will get to it tomorrow. All that tomorrow brings is twice as many messages.

Now, you may be sitting there saying, "I already do this."

Good. But if you do not, start now.

Still, there is more to it than merely replying to clients. You must truly care. Since day one, I have made a habit of returning client phone calls on the same day. This encompasses Monday through Friday and sometimes weekends as well. I estimate that I have missed a same-day callback in less than one percent of all cases in my career.

I reply to emails in as little as one minute, and normally within a few hours. This includes weekends, nights, and most holidays. One client emailed me 127 times since we opened his case. I have sent 97 reply emails. I even text with clients when necessary. I have made it my mission for my clients to never feel ignored.

All we can offer the public is service. If you can't count on service from your lawyers, on what can you count?

"But it is not just the clients—it's also expert witnesses."

I received a call from a top psychologist the other day— one on whom I have relied for expert opinions in various cases.

She commented on how so many attorneys weren't able to pick up the phone for her, despite their requests for her help.

As usual I could only shrug.

What can you say after you hear these things so frequently? This professional is dedicating days on her calendar to appear in court, and lawyers do not even confirm whether they still need her help!

It's inexcusable. They are messing with her calendar, showing her disrespect, and losing a valuable resource for future cases.

There are more problems in this: What if the client loses the case due to the lawyer's inability to secure the witness? That's a major blunder that leads to career downfalls.

Everyone is entitled to callbacks. I recall when I purchased a condo early in my career. It was my first property, and as newlyweds, my wife and I chose a friend, Mike, to do the closing. I did not expect special treatment but by now I am sure you know where this story is going.

Sure enough, whenever we had a question, Mike wouldn't call us back.

The guy not only lost a valuable source of referrals by neglecting us, he also lost a friend. I never requested a discount, and in fact told Mike to bill us as he would any other client. However, I remember really losing my patience with him—because he seemed frustrated with us when we asked normal questions that any first time homebuyers would. I've said it before and will say it again: failure to respond equals poor lawyering which results in the loss of cases, loss of clients, and loss of referrals.

You're serious?

Now, you may be sitting there, shaking your head. "What are you talking about? If I read 100 emails from every client and send 100 replies, I will never get any work done."

First of all, the emails count as part of work. Moreover, this client is the exception. Most of the time, you can manage expectations easily with less communication. The majority of clients are not so high maintenance.

Ultimately, what I am talking about is good service.

A friend was selling her house and located a neighborhood attorney. Let's call him Jones. He quoted her a fee. She retained him. Once hired, Jones ignored her phone calls, so she called me. "I don't understand," my friend commented. "All I want is an answer to a few questions."

I replied that I did not know Jones but offered to contact him. My friend insisted that I need not take time from my schedule.

She said, "I will try one more time and ask his secretary to explain why he hasn't returned my calls. I've been patient, but it's been two weeks, and I left three messages."

I hung up, reminding her once more that I was more than happy to reach out to Jones. Two weeks? Three calls? In my opinion, this treatment was just wrong, especially given my personal obsession with customer service for my immigration clients.

The following week, I heard from my friend. "Well, Mr. Jones finally got back to me."

"And?" I inquired. "Did he tell you what you needed to know?"

"Not exactly," she answered. "He was quite upset. He said that all of my calls were a waste of his time, and that I'm lucky that he doesn't bill me extra."

Now, my friend is a calm sort, a little timid even. I couldn't begin to understand why her lawyer would be angry with her. This Jones had not only upset his client, but he had also failed in his ethical duty to respond. He ignored and then insulted her. He lost an opportunity to impress her with good service.

This attorney also cost himself dozens of potential new cases.

If I am nice to our clients, not only am I doing my job, but I'm also letting them know that I appreciate their business. What is the likelihood that they will recommend me to family and neighbors? In my experience, it's very likely.

All I could tell my friend was, "Sorry that you had such a bad experience. Next time, please ask me if I can give you the name of a colleague who will do the job right."

Doing the job right begins and ends with client service.

And now the secret to being a great attorney

Be very tough on yourself. That's right, I said it. Be your own worst critic. Some of my best law student interns and associates seem to start every sentence with, "This is a really dumb question, but …"

I inevitably tell the licensed ones who set foot in a courtroom that they have six weeks to stop beginning their queries with this preface, but secretly I am happy to hear them say it. Why? It tells me something about them.

Now, perfectionism will kill you if you can never finish an assignment, but the perfectionist who can also master the discipline of time management will be a great lawyer.

So be your own worst critic. Think about losing a case. Worry about it. Lose sleep over your fears that you will never be a success, then prove yourself wrong.

Jesse Ventura was elected governor of Minnesota around the time I had to try one of my most important cases. I remember thinking, "I can win this thing, just like a pro wrestler can become governor of a state." I prepared and then I over-prepared. Heck, I had whittled my direct examination down to an Oscar-winning script.

Then I got to court and about five minutes in, the judge took over the questioning of my client, asked him about a dozen questions, and told the prosecutor he had heard enough. My adversary agreed with the judge, not surprisingly. Twenty minutes later the decision was rendered, the hearing was over, and my client was saved from deportation. He and his family thanked me with tears of relief rolling down their cheeks.

Maybe things would have gone the same way even I had winged it. But I was ready for that case, and that's the part I always remember.

On judges

My first experience of working in the law occurred during the summer of 1992, when I interned in the Civil Court of New York. I traveled over two bridges every morning.

My days were spent with a nice, veteran judge who taught me about the real law. His courtroom seemed so removed from the stuff of casebooks that had dominated the prior nine months of my life.

On a day in early July, I sat in a tiny conference area observing my first honest-to-goodness settlement conference. While I was far from naïve, I was still surprised to hear a disbarred attorney argue with my judge, even calling him by his first name to his face.

The judge, nonplussed but calm, just sat for a few minutes, and then walked out, summoning me along with him.

Once outside, the judge whispered to me, "Find my senior clerk and tell him to go in there, please. Those guys don't leave until they make a deal. I have more important things to do."

One of the other memories I have from that summer was how the judge ran his docket. He sat on the bench with me in an empty witness box, right next to him. Often he would lean over and talk to me about "shooting-from-the-hip justice." Occasionally we would talk about baseball as attorneys moved around.

Still, time was at a premium.

The young lawyers approached, ready to argue motions, and

he would politely cut them off. "You have five minutes to tell me everything. Go."

The older attorneys knew the drill. They kept it concise.

Could I go back to law school that fall and try this out in Moot Court? No. They would give me an F. But it sure gave me a great perspective on the real world.

An intern in my office worked for the late Judge Joseph Falcone, a judge who is remembered for making cases in New Jersey Superior Court speedier. She told me that one of the most unique and beneficial experiences that she had in his courtroom was watching the sentencings.

Judge Falcone would not only accomplish the legal formalities required for a sentencing, but he would connect on a personal level with the defendants. One male, addicted to heroin, was being sentenced for another possession offense. The man had a significant criminal history as a result of his addiction. The man had his family sitting behind him in the courtroom. The judge pointed at his family. He told him that he needed to take responsibility for his family, and most importantly, his actions.

That kind of person leaves a legacy.

If law were music, sometimes it would sing joyful songs

A lawyer at my firm, Lauren, won a case. Consequently, a man—brought here lawfully as a child—was allowed to remain in the United States. He rejoined his family.

If things had gone differently, he would have been deported. The man would have had little to no chance of ever returning to America, despite the fact that in his case, the punishment for the offense had included no jail time.

Still, in our phase of the proceedings, the federal government put our client in mandatory detention.

Here are the words that this man's mother wrote to my associate, Lauren:

"Thank you so much for all you did, God Bless you.

I will be sending you blessings every single day so you continue helping people and bringing happiness to more families the way you did with us.

You are an Amazing Attorney!!"

Lauren emailed me: "Our colleagues wonder why I can do so much detention work... Who wouldn't want that kind of gratitude from their clients?"

You work your hardest to win for that kind of gratitude. Knowing that what you have done is appreciated, and that you made a positive difference in your client's life, makes your work worth it.

Unless someone like you cares a whole awful lot, nothing is going to get better. It's not.

Dr. Seuss, *The Lorax*

Slowing down and saving time

One of the best things to do when making adjustments to your life, is to slow down. People in our society are always in a rush. They drive too fast. They fly through the channels on their remote control. Ever see people walking on a busy city street at rush hour?

The syndrome is so prevalent that we now purchase cars on the internet and flip houses as quickly as possible.

The problem is, as the saying goes, "Speed kills."

Going too fast means you cannot possibly calm down. If you are always in a hurry, chances are that your excuse is that you are "too busy to slow down." I do not accept this belief. There is a huge difference between saving time and running, simply because you find it hard to relax.

I have a relative, Al, who is always in a rush. Duke used to say that Al was "always hurrying to go nowhere." And that is the real problem in our world. You sprint all day to get to the next thing.

If you have to be at a business meeting on time, give yourself extra time to get there. Schedule your appointments in a way that does not compromise your time, so that you are not constantly trying to catch up. Use a smartphone or the old-fashioned daily planner, and stick with your plans. The mere addition of a calendar is a wonderful way to change your life. It may sound like common sense to some, but I have seen a great many professionals who work without a formal schedule.

Return your emails and phone calls every day, so that you do not have double the amount to deal with the next day. Open your mail as soon as you get it. Use electronic transfers to pay bills and directly deposit earnings whenever feasible to save time.

When you drive, keep your car at the speed limit. Trust me, you will get there. Speeding increases the risk of accidents for yourself and others. Allot yourself more time, which usually means simply getting up earlier. Driving like an idiot ensures traffic tickets, fines, higher insurance bills, and maybe even hospitalization or death.

Excessive speeds cannot help your blood pressure. A guy gave me the finger recently, and I told him at the next red light, "Thanks. Guys like you—with your anger problems—help feed a lot of lawyers' families."

Admittedly, some people hate to be late for events. So, like I said already, leave earlier. And if your life is just so hectic that you do not have possibly enough hours in the day to handle all of your duties, it is time to sit down and make a budget. Not a budget for finances, but one for your time. Figure out what you absolutely need to do, then subtract those duties that are optional.

Now, I know what you may say. You're thinking, "Nothing in my life is optional."

I do not buy this for one second.

I will bet anything that you are wasting hours every day on certain activities—particularly minutes or hours spent aimlessly watching TV or surfing the net, or doing something else that amuses you.

Diversions need to be limited, because they interfere with your ability to take care of your true responsibilities.

And speaking of responsibility, when you move too fast, your judgment can become clouded. I do not know how many times I have heard people lament over mistakes that could have been avoided if they had been patient in their preparations. So, again, slow down, especially before making a huge decision.

What do I recommend you do with your free time? Unlike the aforementioned habits of television and the web, there are productive ways to spend free time. Try reading literature, history, science, or philosophy. You will feel like you have actually accomplished something and benefit by keeping your mind sharp.

Yoga is a nice way to relax and work hard simultaneously; it will definitely change your life to become more flexible, focus on your breathing and just feel plain *better*. I know more than one lawyer who has become a yoga instructor.

Laughter is really good for you. Laughing has been shown to be healthy for the heart, circulation, and immune system. It will reduce stress and anxiety. So listen to some podcasts or YouTube comedy routines.

There are the classics, like Richard Pryor and George Carlin. A current favorite of mine is Bill Burr. If you prefer clean humor, Brian Regan is an outstanding comedian who never swears.

Half our life is spent trying to find something to do with the time we have rushed through life trying to save.

Will Rogers

One thousand dollars

I recall one old lawyer, Abe, once telling me a long time ago: "I don't pick up a phone for a client unless I get a thousand dollars." His point, of course, was that if you don't get a retainer, clients take advantage of your charitable side.

My take on this is that different circumstances call for different approaches.

I've observed that some not-for-profit agencies, which used to refer work to private firms, keep the cases.

Only trouble is, in many of those offices, they are understaffed and have no resources, so their clients suffer.

Moreover, I have been told repeatedly by a lot of folks at nonprofits that it is accepted that their clients often can afford private counsel.

So what gives?

There is desperation out there—shared equally by attorneys in both public and private settings, as well as their clients—to hang on to money. Some people who can afford a higher fee still try to get a low-cost agency in lieu of a law firm. The attorneys at these entities, funded by grants, are under pressure to demonstrate that they have plenty of work. Thus they maintain a larger client base than they can handle, even if it means that they are not going to return phone calls until a week or two later.

We all have free will. Nobody can force someone to pay a fee that he deems too high. I am amazed sometimes at how people will haggle over costs when they have family in jail, but that's human nature.

On the other hand, we all know that there are wealthy people who want expensive attorneys engaged to perform services at the highest fees, almost as a status symbol ("My lawyer bills me $900 an hour"). The thing I find intriguing about that scenario is that some attorneys are absolutely worth such rates, while others remind me of Bernie Madoff. The trick is to know the difference.

As the late Sy Syms reminded us in his TV commercials, "An educated consumer is our best customer." My clients often have done plenty of research before calling for a consultation. It's a compliment to me, but I also know that they will expect not only top service but also reasonable fees.

I am happy to oblige.

Never, ever yell

What is it about so many lawyers that makes them feel obligated or entitled to yell? They scream at their staff and their clients. What the devil are they thinking?

Consider this: People walk into your business with money, ready to pay you to help them. Do you (a) smile and take the fee, or (b) yell at them, so they are so turned off that they never want to see you again, and (c) will not tell anyone they know to hire you? Do the math.

The office also is not a happy environment if the boss yells. I made a promise to myself years ago not to raise my voice at my team. I heard so many awful stories about these partners who brutalized their associates and paralegals and secretaries—what could be the reason? To scare them into doing a better job? To make them despise the workplace?

Law firms are not NFL teams. We are not here to work on the proper way to sack the quarterback.

Now I know some of you will say, "Yeah, but figuratively speaking, attorneys do need to tackle the opposition."

Fine.

I still think it's bad strategy. It reminds me of an old coach I had. He yelled and cussed, and his teams won. He may have even cared about his players but we were high school kids. That sort of approach does not work well with adults, unless they are being paid to collide violently with other human beings.

Have fun

Many, many years ago, the only diversion that got in the way of good service from lawyers was golf. At least that's what one lawyer wrote in a book I once stumbled upon, on how to build a law practice in the 1970s.

Today, there are a myriad of distractions. It does not matter whether you would rather read non-work related e-mails, use social media, watch TV, read books, listen to music, or even play golf. And those of us who have children will always have the legitimate excuse that we need to spend more time with our kids.

Which raises an important point.

In my experience, adults are no different from children. Given our way, we would all prefer to have fun. The city of Las Vegas operates on this premise, as do New Orleans and Orlando.

In the end, it comes down to focus, and the use of that focus to resist the temptations that life throws at us. Decide on an area that you wish to pursue. Choose something that you love. Then go for it with everything you have got. Immerse yourself in an area, not unlike a young medical student who chooses a specialty. There's a saying that if you find something you love to do that you can get paid for, you will never work a day in your life. Practicing law is no different. Find a specialty that intrigues you, and learn everything you can about it.

The more time you can devote to learning to practice in one area of law, the more likely it will be that you will find work and clients whom you can help.

You may be unsure whether this advice is likely to work in real life, particularly if you work in an established practice.

"How can I change my focus?" I hear you ask.

First, let me pose this question: Do you like what you do? If you don't, it's time to do some serious thinking.

If you are still a student, or unemployed, it's easier to choose something you love. For the rest of you, I still firmly believe that the magic solution will work just as easily. Here's how to do it: make it your hobby, or do some pro bono work. I have a few pro bono cases going now for young people with no money, as well as military personnel, not to mention a man afflicted with a life-threatening illness, and a human trafficking victim too.

There are so many areas today that are screaming for talented, motivated, dedicated attorneys. You just need to match your interests with the work. Think of it as one of those online dating services. It may take time. But that's okay. Six months from now, after you finish this book, and if you follow its instructions, you may have fallen in love again—or for the first time ever.

And what about those of you who are, quite frankly, either burnt out or unhappy with what you do for a living? Well, you have nothing to lose by trying to follow my advice. The worst-case scenario is that you will end up having taken on a new goal.

The best-case scenario, which I believe firmly will occur, is that you will be more successful and happier than you have been in years.

I don't care how old you are. Your gender, political beliefs; if you're married or single; gay or straight; you need to lose 15 pounds, or believe that you are perfect already.

You wouldn't be reading this if you didn't think there was room for improvement in the way you can practice law. We all can get better.

As for those of you considering law school, or already enrolled, this advice is just as helpful. Quite frankly, my own career satisfaction is largely due to the fact that I followed this advice about twenty years ago.

In law school I first discovered immigration law. It fascinated me and there were other people doing the same thing. One guy in my class was interested in working in pro football— people thought he was crazy. After all, getting a job in sports as an attorney is not much easier than getting a job playing for a team. The talent pool is deep.

But this guy was focused. As the story goes, he went down to the Dome and volunteered to do anything that the team needed. Photocopying, emptying garbage cans, filing, you name it. He met people. Eventually the guy demonstrated his expertise in understanding nuances of sports law such as managing a salary cap and negotiating contracts with agents.

My former classmate was general manager of an NFL team in a major market for half a dozen years.

Try to do things that other people think are impossible

As the former UFC middleweight champion Anderson Silva said, "I don't think I'm the best. I just try to do things that other people think are impossible." It's not just how you think about yourself. It's a healthy approach to anything you do; I try to instill this in the people who work at my firm. I've certainly learned a lot from all of them, too.

I had three law students interning with me one semester, and they were all great. One of them noticed a small but incredibly important legal issue in a federal appeal that we are handling. That issue was crucial in winning the case.

Anybody can be the best. But to try to do the impossible— that's an even more impressive goal.

Piano and law

My son took up piano at age six. He's very good. He's in fifth grade now and has played live to audiences in public places. He knows the key of any song he hears, immediately. He sight reads. He memorizes pieces and he can sit down at the piano and replicate any tune he just heard— plus throw in improvisational sections.

Back when this all became apparent, it was all the more obvious that we needed a keyboard. So we went shopping on a Saturday morning after his karate class. Off we went, rolling down Route 17, one of the greatest highways for retail shopping in the United States.

The first place we tried was a music store, a big place that was filled with a ton of instruments and exactly no customers when we arrived.

I brought Owen over to check out a $600 electronic piano. He played it for all of two minutes before the salesman approached us.

What was immediately clear was that my kid was "on the clock," as they say about pro golfers who take too much time over their shots. Basically, he had about two more minutes to play before we had to decide if we wanted to buy.

The dude even gave us the "OK... that's enough" after Owen played another song.

"Yeah, that *is* enough," I thought to myself. "You just cost yourself a customer."

Before parenthood and the wisdom that comes with it, I might have replied with a curse word or two. Instead I just thanked the guy and left him, alone, in an empty, giant room filled with beautiful musical instruments all begging for someone to play them.

Not long afterwards, we found ourselves in a Steinway showroom. Owen sat at a grand piano. I asked the manager if he could try it out, especially since the price tag was $115,000.

"Sure," said the man, "what's he going to do? Break it?" He laughed.

I almost laughed too.

Instead I thought, "Yeah, maybe my kid will break your extraordinarily expensive piano."

Owen opened up with Minuet in G. Then he played the blues, some ragtime, and Mozart. He jammed, too. Before we knew it, an hour must have gone by. The employees never bothered us.

We did not buy the piano, as it was a little pricey and a tad early in Owen's career but I will never forget that day.

I juxtaposed the pleasant atmosphere of the Steinway store with that of the first place. What I take away from that Saturday morning is how impatient the guy was in the first shop. He reminded me of far too many professionals I know: burnt out. Age may play a factor in this syndrome, but I do not even think that is the real problem.

Patience is necessary when dealing with the public. So what can you do? Smile. It's a simple rule. Listen to them, whether they're playing the piano or telling you their problems.

I have an associate who said that when she first started with me, she could not believe how long I would let some consultations run. My reply was concise. "The longer I listen, the greater the likelihood they might want to retain us."

Too many lawyers watch the clock. It's not their fault. They were raised on hourly billing. Only the thing is, time is not our only asset.

I have had occasion to sit in on consultations with a top personal injury practitioner. One meeting ran over five hours. Even for me, that took some patience, but it was an excellent learning experience.

Arrogance

The public has a certain perception about the legal profession. Attorneys are often considered to be arrogant. Admittedly, it is difficult to walk the fine line between ego and humility when we are expected to win cases with life-altering consequences.

But consider this: I once consulted with a man with a very difficult case. Nothing new about that. But an aspect of what happened was very educational to me as an attorney.

I asked all of my questions and reviewed his papers. He kept pointing to one section of one page. It was a commonly generated notice of action from a government agency.

I responded that I had seen this language thousands of times. I did not bother to read the thing word for word, rather jumping for law books to support my initial conclusions about how to resolve the case.

Finally, when I reentered my office, I sat down and looked at the paper, which was still in the center of my desk. The man sat silently as I finally read the document. And wouldn't you know it? There were some sentences in there that I had never seen before—important stuff that might help solve his problem.

I was so caught up in analysis that I glossed over the diagnosis. In other words, ego got in the way. Luckily, I returned to the important lesson that I had learned from my days of training in Brazilian Jiu-Jitsu, which I often apply to the law:

"What's the key to ground fighting? What should I focus on? The answer, when it comes from Zé or Murilo, is enlightening: humility. Always assume that your opponent is better than you and that he knows more—you have to work harder in training and learn more. You know only five percent of what there is to know. Fight your own pride and ego, and be open-minded and always learning new techniques, new things from anyone."

Excerpt from *A Fighter's Heart* by Sam Sheridan

The thing is, I just found out that I had been named to *Best Lawyers in America* for the tenth year in a row, and that sort of honor is humbling.

And yet, I never want to let the awards go to my head. Instead, I want to remember that I only know five percent of what there is to know, because just like ground fighting, the law is a never-ending series of combinations and confusing twists.

And it requires focus on humility.

I learned the answer to this fellow's problem, not by reading it in a statute or sharing information with my colleagues, although those elements are crucial as well. The answer was staring me right in the face.

"99 percent of lawyers give the rest a bad name." – Steven Wright

The legal profession really could use a major overhaul, like one of those HGTV shows where someone renovates a house.

Lawyers are often referred to as sharks, shysters, or even ambulance chasers; take your pick of pejoratives. They are frequently viewed as putting money first and clients last.

One proposal to change public perception of attorneys would be for state bar associations to designate more specialties and certify those lawyers interested in pursuing those practice areas through courtroom hours and continuing legal education coursework.

This plan would accomplish multiple goals. Attorneys, as

I have noted, will always have a greater likelihood of success by narrowing the focus of their practice. Moreover, much like certain physicians filling the medical needs of their patients, attorneys could solve the problems of their clients by staying in one section of the law.

When people ask me what I do for a living, if I answer, "Lawyer," there is a relatively good chance that I will hear a joking comment about how our profession is all about billing—the obvious implication being that we are greedy.

However, when I reply, "Immigration lawyer," the listener immediately starts discussing policy with me. The conversation turns to how folks in my field help foreign nationals and their American relatives.

Think about it for a minute. The same holds true whether you say, "Bankruptcy practitioner," "Matrimonial lawyer," "Civil litigator," or "Patent attorney."

People start talking about the service we provide, not the cash we collect.

And speaking of humility...

One thing that has always driven me crazy is "lawyer speak." I am not talking about when attorneys need to use terminology that is required in our day-to-day functioning with each other. Instead, I mean the silly habit that some counselors pick up, when they use fancy words to try to impress clients.

It's not always their fault. In the legal profession, the jargon permeates the syntax that they drill into your head all through law school.

But let's be real for a second. When you meet someone at the office, do you find yourself using words that you know are over his head? If so, consider why. Is it necessary?

One word that may have been beaten to death recently is "transparent." However, it is appropriate to use the word "transparent" when we talk to clients. The way I see it, nobody should walk out of my office asking: "What did he just say?"

Throwing around a few old-school Latin phrases may be one way to demonstrate your expertise. Then again, it is more likely to turn people off. I would not wish to consult a surgeon who couldn't explain the procedure in plain English. By the same token, I would not hire a lawyer who walked me through the case with a bunch of legal psychobabble.

Nobody should ever have to leave the office confused by an attorney who, even unintentionally, intimidates folks into hiring him with the use of unnecessary jargon.

Take pride in your work

Sometimes when confronted with the general indifference that afflicts so many lawyers, I wonder what would happen to them if they actually took pride in their work.

You see this sort of thing with a great woodworker, for example. Ever watch a guy complete the perfect built-in bookshelf? Ever notice how satisfied he is when the job is done? Sure, there are many attorneys who put that kind of effort into their cases, and nothing feels better than winning. But I am talking about true passion, like when you see a great cook present a wonderful dish.

There is something very satisfying about finishing certain projects.

My theory is that a fighting spirit is not part of many lawyers' everyday approaches. And that is a shame. People's lives are often on the line. As significant as the furniture or meal is to the artisans I mentioned above, what about the human being who is directly affected by your dedication?

We all must look in the mirror, like fighters in the gym. Find some pride. Bring it into the office.

Umphrey's Law

Imagine, if you will, a six-partner law firm in the city of Chicago. The core members first met at Notre Dame. Along the way some guys joined, one from DePaul and another from an elite school in Boston. They are specialists— perhaps the only legal team in America that attracts a certain type of client.

Now imagine that the same law firm will do a weeklong seminar in a stunning, rustic setting. They will meet with clients, law students, and peers in both workshops and independent meetings. The fee for the week will be very reasonable.

In reality, we are not talking about a law practice. Instead, the six-man outfit is a musical group. They are known as Umphrey's McGee. In fact, while the original band formed at Notre Dame, one guy has a Master's degree in jazz drumming from DePaul, and another studied guitar at the prestigious Berklee College of Music.

The way this band performs resonates with me deeply; they have been around for more than fifteen years with a solid work ethic and fine educations forming the backbone of their success. And as is often the case, the students become teachers.

Indeed, Umphrey's holds a week of classes, private lessons, and performances in upstate New York. The event is called "sUMmer school." Rather than selling tickets to an audience, they charge a flat rate to attend this unique experience.

As a lawyer, I am constantly studying ways in which the wall can be broken between two parties in a professional relationship, to bring them closer together.

I am impressed by how Umphrey's McGee is removing the "fan" label from a segment of the quarter million or so Facebook fans they have, by inviting the first 150 of that group who applies to matriculate to sUMmer school.

It is interesting that—after I reported the news of legal education seminars I moderated—many followers of my law firm on Facebook made requests to attend such events in the future. My immediate reply was to say that the programs were mandated by state law, and I simply volunteered to put them together for other attorneys.

Nonetheless, I took something away from both Umphrey's and my own "audience."

So, now, in addition to lecturing to audiences of fellow attorneys, I speak to other groups, from parents at elementary schools to various ethnic organizations.

I had a group of buddies in college, and we all thought that the three best things in life were drinking beer, meeting women, and eating pizza. When we got together after our first semester of law school, we agreed that the three best things in life were reading magazines, drinking soda, and watching television.

First message from above paragraph: Expectations change with responsibility.

Second message: Television can be a powerful drug. There is a scene in the film *The Paper Chase*, in which Harvard Law students seek refuge in a hotel room to study for finals. One of them tells the bellman, "Get that damn thing out of here."

Of course, he is pointing towards the television set.

The same rule goes for lawyers. When I am not at the office, I try to avoid television. Sure, I will have a ball game on in the background, or might have a favorite show, but if you fall into a pattern of constantly having TV on, you will be far less productive. The projects pile up, and long-awaited success somehow eludes you.

I made a list of my favorite shows not long ago: *Hill Street Blues*, *MASH*, *Sopranos*, *WKRP*, *The White Shadow*, *Seinfeld*, *The A Team*, *Entourage*.

What did I discover? Except for two recent cable TV hits, all of my top programs aired in my time between junior high and college.

TV is a waste of time, in excess. If I view many programs, will I have time to plan out the various Continuing Legal Education Seminars I have conducted? Would I have had found the hours it took to write this book?

And would I have discovered what is truly valuable to me, outside of my work?

Equality

Hüsker Dü was my favorite band in high school.

The whole world wasn't ready for their sound in the 80s, but there was a faithful audience for bands like Hüsker Dü. Kids like me would pack clubs like Irving Plaza and the old Ritz in NYC.

What I remember vividly about this band, beyond the music, was how after gigs, their bass player, Greg Norton, stood outside the venues, and shook hands with the fans.

I've written about how Umphrey's McGee has broken down the wall between the stars of the show and the audience. Similarly, the law firm should not look at its clients as somehow beneath the status of lawyers.

Greg Norton was one of the first and, more than 25 years later, only musicians I've met who wasn't on an ego trip.

Clients constantly say how they really like talking to me. I always tell them, "What you see is what you get." When other attorneys behave as if they are superior to the folks who pay them for services rendered, that's unfortunate.

I must have consulted with a thousand people over the last

year, folks who express how comfortable they are with how I act towards them. These are the same ones who communicate their dissatisfaction with the supercilious lawyers who talked down to them, or yelled at them, or ignored them.

I learned how to be nice to the people with whom I interact was to subconsciously imitate a guy from a rock group whose lyrics I quoted in my high school yearbook.

But the clients want someone to make them feel safe, don't they?

Yes, and you can accomplish this task without acting superior towards them. You have every right to bring confidence into a courthouse or negotiation room. You shouldn't stop trying to be the best in your chosen speciality. Remember, be dumb, know that you are dumb, and that will make you smart.

Still, I firmly believe that you will ascend to greater heights by remembering that you are not better than your client.

How to deal with unhappy clients

It's part of the business. Inevitably, some clients will communicate their frustrations to you.

If you follow my previous advice about responsiveness and care for client needs, you can avoid much of this. Still, you cannot make everyone happy all the time.

So what do you do?

Say you get a nasty email or phone call. The client is displeased with how things are going in his case, although it may have absolutely nothing to do with your efforts.

Step One: Hear him out. Let him rant. Don't say a word until he's clearly finished venting.

Step Two: Pause before responding. Speak in a quiet, calm, slow, measured manner. If the communication is written, do not impulsively bang out an angry retort, but let the email sit for a little while. Do reply, however, because your silence will only make him madder.

Step Three: Express your empathy for his case, even if he behaves in a manner that you would ordinarily deem offensive.

Step Four: Remind him that you are on his side. You're no happier about his plight than he is. You're an advocate, and you hate losing.

Step Five: Resist the urge to argue, yell, or shout him down.

Step Six: Let him know that you are doing everything you can to fix the situation.

Step Seven: Explain that this type of situation is very rare. Say that 99 percent of your clients are satisfied with your work, but you strive for 100 percent.

By the time you are done following Steps 1-7, chances are that you will have defused the drama.

Clients like this hypothetical one are similar to drivers with road rage. When you get flipped the bird on a highway, let the madman speed away. Decelerate your vehicle until you cannot see him anymore. Option to talk with him at next red light.

Fight for your right!

In the film *Rocky Balboa*, the hero comes out of retirement to have a fight for the title against a much younger champion.

It's pretty well established that Sly Stallone got his inspiration from watching 45-year-old George Foreman knock out the then-heavyweight champion Michael Moorer, who at the time was all of age 26. This accomplishment stands out in boxing history.

I watched that Foreman fight with my dad, and it happened to take place just a few months after I received my law degree. Suffice it to say, we were both rooting for the older fighter.

My dad was not one given to cheerful displays of emotion, but when Foreman won, he actually jumped up and high fived me.

I found myself watching *Rocky Balboa* on DVD with my son, age nine, as I was begrudgingly admitting to myself that I was actually 43 years of age. By the end I didn't feel so old.

There's an extraordinarily inspirational moment in the film. The father tells his son (and later reminds himself):

"It ain't about how hard you hit, it's about how you can get hit and keep moving forward. How much you can take and keep moving forward."

So there it is, for attorneys who have been going to war in courtrooms, or negotiating, or any other advocacy for their clients, whether you've been practicing for five years or fifty.

If you've been down on yourself for whatever reason, whether it's the economy, or that burnout that hits many lawyers at some point. Stop.

Think about fighting— not for your clients, but for *you*.

This goes back to when the father of a friend of mine, a very nice gentleman who spent a lifetime in the advertising industry, cautioned me about using the clichéd phrase 'fighting for our clients' to promote my law firm.

I took his point and stayed away from the language.

But this story of Rocky Balboa is not about fighting for your client. It's about fighting for you.

A never-say-die attitude can get you very far in your legal career. How much you can get hit and keep moving forward, indeed.

I learn something from talking to anyone, listening to someone, and observing everyone.

The security guard who works the late shift? That man is always smiling and pleasant. He could grumble about working in solitary conditions all night, but he's never anything but cheerful.

The young lady who carefully chose flowers for my wife and daughter? She took her time, selected the best roses and daisies, chatted with me about various topics, and before I left the florist, asked me for my business card. She even complimented the design and logo.

The clients who come in day after day? They tell me tales of suffering, sometimes the worst experiences you could imagine. But they're resilient and will do anything they have to do, just to survive.

The man I know who has practiced law for 55 years?

I ask, "How are you?"

He answers, "Any day above the grass beats a day beneath it."

What can you say after that?

Attitude will carry you a long way. For yourself, for your career, and for the impression that you leave on others.

Rickey's gonna get it

This comes from fifteen-year veteran baseball player Brent Mayne's blog. Here is what the former major leaguer and author of *The Art of Catching* had to say about one of my role models, Rickey Henderson.

"The cool thing about Rickey, though, was that he never complained to the umps. Instead, he would talk to himself in the third person. An umpire would call a ball way outside for a strike, Rickey would jump back and start yapping, 'OK now, Rickey can't hit that pitch… Rickey's good but not that good.' Stuff like that. He was amazing, the words never stopped. He actually talked to himself… as the pitch was coming. The pitch was in mid-flight and you could hear him say, 'Rickey's gonna get it.'"

"Rickey's gonna get it."

As a lawyer, I do not know how many times I have thought of that quotation in my legal career, but it is quite instructive.

The power, through positivity, to believe that you can do something, is amazing.

For those of you non-baseball followers, Rickey Henderson

is the greatest leadoff hitter and base runner of all time. He has more stolen bases, runs, unintentional walks, and leadoff home runs than any player in major league history.

It's a one-in-a-million shot to make the majors, a major accomplishment by itself. But Rickey was the best in a whole bunch of areas.

I have walked into many courtrooms, saying, "I'm gonna get it." And that's what each and every lawyer should do. Not just for themselves, but for the client too.

Laziness

The biggest problem is that many lawyers are not doing as well for their clients as they could. Why? They just don't want to work that hard.

I will never forget the initial time I went inside the courthouse after I was admitted to the bar. The first lawyer I met was a grizzled turkey. His sage words to me were (and I swear this is true), "Nice to meet you, kid; this is easy money."

I nodded and kept my mouth shut.

My attitude today is the same as it was then, two decades ago. Nothing should ever be easy. After making appearances and seeing clients and reviewing documents, I would go home, try to see my kids as much as possible, then after they went to sleep, instead of watching TV, I would blog, tweet, and post on my law firm's Facebook page, then work on other internet projects to promote my practice. I would prepare and present lectures and seminars for Continuing Legal Education organizations.

To be the best is to work the hardest. If you spend your free time doing what you love and working the hardest at it, even if you aren't the smartest, you can and will come out on top.

Shortcuts don't cut it

Did you use Cliff's Notes when you were in high school? Or did you actually read the books?

Which option worked better to increase your vocabulary and writing skills? Certainly when you read the book you had a better sense of the characters. You could imagine how they spoke by the way the book was written.

One disturbing trend that has emerged in recent years among lawyers is using list servs and other email discussion groups to get the Cliff's Notes version of how to handle cases.

It wasn't that long ago when lawyers had to read statutes and cases to learn post-law school. Most attorneys still go this route and supplement their continuing legal education by attending seminars.

But I'm on several list servs, I have noticed more and more lawyers simply asking, "How do you do a _____ ?"

What do I think of that approach?

Lazy.

Won't help you be a better lawyer.

Won't help your firm.

Won't help your clients.

Won't help your reputation.

The original idea behind these Internet mailing lists, for various legal communities, as I recall, was to share names of folks for referrals, as well as offering mentoring and promoting advocacy.

But as of late, they have become a mechanism for avoiding research. What's missing is the sense of the law. You get more than just the headnotes when you actually do the research. You get the reasoning, the policy—all of the things you need to advocate strongly.

It's truly a shame. Everyone suffers. The quality of legal representation diminishes.

When we were grade schoolers, we all had a teacher who replied to students' queries on what a word meant by handing them a dictionary.

Today, we've become so accustomed to googling, that at some point, it became acceptable to some folks to replace thorough research with email blasting several hundred peers with what are often the most fundamental legal questions.

There's always a colleague willing to tell a fellow lawyer how to do a case. That person may think that he's being a nice guy, but his good intentions result in attorneys not being educated properly. And who suffers most? The clients? The lawyer? How about both?

Whenever I see a post criticizing this practice of shortcutting, inevitably half a dozen defensive replies emerge quickly.

1. "You have to learn somehow!"
2. "Who are you to tell others they can't ask questions?"
3. "What's wrong with helping?"
4. "Arrogant, aren't you?"
5. "Why don't you just hit delete if you don't want to participate?"
6. "You know, we all have to start out!"

Problem is, it's the wrong way to learn, and it's not helping if the lawyers fail to grasp the real law.

Things are so bad that I heard a story of a judge who told a would-be litigator to go home and read Civil Procedure again.

Have some pride in your work. Be a better practitioner. Study. Pull up law review articles. Become an expert.

Don't just collect a fee and tell yourself, "I will go on a list serv and ask how to do this case." Once you cross that line, next thing you know, you will never practice law the right way.

Instead of shortcutting, try looking for a good mentor.

Know people

A buddy of mine, Nick, tells a story of a modern pop icon who was in the market for a $50 million penthouse. It goes like this:

One day, the hugely successful music star (let's call him "Charlie Freak") parked his Rolls Royce outside the brand new development where the apartment was situated.

Charlie Freak and his assistants headed to the elevator and began inspecting the premises.

Not long after, the real estate impresario in charge of this burgeoning project pulled into the lot. He left his Rolls nearby, saw the same car on his way into the building and raised his eyebrows.

A potential buyer? Nice.

Now, the builder was a fellow in his mid-seventies and not exactly up on the latest music. When he entered the penthouse, he was greeted by his staff but blew past them and introduced himself personally to the interested party.

The developer never got a chance to discover who the star was. So, instead of talking real business with Charlie Freak, the older gentleman spent a great deal of time sizing him up. How did the would-be purchaser of this property earn enough to afford it, he thought? He was an athlete of some sort, or perhaps a drug dealer?

Finally, one of the employees grabbed him casually with an excuse to get him away long enough to identify the star.

The magnate knew the name Charlie Freak, but not the face or his work. Immediately after this conversation occurred, the singer was approached by a member of his own organization who had been eavesdropping.

Amused that the builder had just been debriefed as to his identity, Charlie Freak was reported to have uttered, "This mother must be really rich if he hasn't heard of me."

Lesson: know people. I am not advocating that you scour celebrity gossip sites *per se*, but at least try to have a clue who people are—not merely famous individuals, but learn about everyone you meet. It sounds simple, but most people don't do their homework. I frequently look at my potential clients' emails to me to see what they need; then I might Google them, or check out their LinkedIn, Facebook, or Twitter pages.

When I meet with potential clients, I know that they have spent time researching me online. Why shouldn't I do the same?

I'm not going down anymore

As noted above, I showed my kids the *Rocky* movies, and they're big fans as a result. There's a scene in which Rocky gets knocked down for what is apparently the thousandth time in his career. And the fight he's in, it's like the most important one of his life.

Anyhow he gets back up, as usual, and finishes the round. But there's this amazing moment when—back in the corner—he says to his trainer, "I'm not going down anymore."

I have always loved that line. It inspires me so much as a lawyer, an advocate, and a representative of so many people with major problems—folks who rely on my team and me to fix those problems and get their lives straightened out.

Fall down ten times, one old martial arts saying advises, then get up eleven times.

Rocky took it one step further. He said, "I'm not going down anymore."

Shut up, Counselor

Many years ago I sat in a courtroom in Philadelphia, waiting for the judge. The only other person present was the prosecutor, sitting quietly across from me.

My client was in a prison far away in front of a camera, to be heard that day by television monitor.

The judge soon entered. He sat down at his bench and began to read his file, ignoring the other lawyer and me. We were all waiting for the jail to send word that the camera was hooked up, as the signal was down for the moment.

Finally I whispered something to my adversary about the case, just to pass the time. Before she could answer, the judge looked up and uttered three words that I had never heard before: "Shut up, Counselor."

I was incredulous. But what could I do? I shut up.

I later found out that this judge was notorious.

The City Council overwhelmingly passed a resolution calling for his removal from the bench, years after he told me to shut up. Seems that a federal appeals court ruled that he failed to give fair and impartial hearings, referring to a pattern of "belligerent questioning and a failure to consider relevant evidence," "brow-beating," and "nitpicking" by the judge.

But I still shut up at the time. I was a young lawyer in a courtroom in a city in which I rarely appeared, and I had a client to defend. At the time, my only thought was trying to win the case. Avoiding getting on the judge's bad side seemed like a good idea. I only later found out that he did not have much of a good side. But such is life.

If you litigate, you know that things can get ugly sometimes. All you can do is remember that you have little to do with the attitude and behavior of the other parties in the room.

The Shakespearean maxim about discretion being the better part of valor made sense to me then. It still does now.

Sometimes you shut up.

And sometimes you talk.

A lot.

Lecturing

Practicing law well and lecturing is hard work, but it pays off for a number of reasons.

» You benefit your community by providing them a continuing legal education to help their clients.

» You develop yourself, because speaking requires you to keep up with the latest developments in your specialty.

» You help your clients as you ensure that you have left no stone unturned in the handling of their cases.

» You do a good deed, as you become known for volunteering your time to help others.

» You elevate your standing by establishing yourself as an expert whose advice is solicited by peers.

» You strengthen your business, as many people want the

best lawyer. And a top professional is generally sought after by those in need.

I have enjoyed lecturing immensely. It feels good to talk to audiences of colleagues. I liken it to the rush that performers must feel when doing a concert.

When I have moderated five-hour panels on different aspects of my area, immigration law, I often review the seminars with the other speakers. We often feel like a band that has just left the stage after putting on a great show.

Bring some interest to work to beat boredom

Most attorneys' major complaint is how boring their jobs are.

My initial response to that is that we have air conditioning in the summer and heat in the winter at our offices, so things could be a lot worse.

Still, getting interested in your work sometimes takes effort. Personally, I think dealing with people is fun—especially from all over the world. That's a big attraction of my work.

Once in law school, I attended a sports law lecture given by an NBA executive named Ed Tapscott (lawyer turned pro sports coach) who told us, "If you want to work in our industry, then go to work, but if you're just a fan, stay a fan."

His point was, choose wisely.

But you can always take a step back if you ended up in an office bored out your mind. There is always a way to find interest if you take a new perspective. Get to know your clients better. Find things about them that interest you.

We live in a society that emphasizes how "notable" a tiny percentage of people are. Those folks are featured in *People* and *Sports Illustrated* and *TIME*. Chances are, most—if not all—of your clients are not on any magazine covers.

Just because your clients aren't big stars doesn't mean they're boring.

And even more important is the bottom line. My late father-in-law, Mort, worked in the film industry for many years. Back in the day, it was not unusual for Robert Redford or Paul Newman to visit the offices where he edited film. Yet he never found himself star struck.

"They get up in the morning and put their pants on, just like we do," Mort would exclaim, when asked about how exciting his work with movie actors must be.

So whether you are easily impressed by fame or couldn't care less, go beyond the initial images of your clients. Get to know them well. The better you can relate to them, the more interest you will take in their lives and their problems.

Q: What makes a great lawyer?

A: Never forgetting why you started out in the first place.

If it's because you truly love the law, and advocacy—wonderful.

If it's to help people—great.

If it's to make money, hey, we all have families (and employees) who need to eat.

If it's to create jobs, well, then you need to grow that firm.

If it's to try to change the world, go for it.

Me? I would probably say "All of the above."

CPSIA information can be obtained at www.ICGtesting.com
Printed in the USA
BVOW08s1334100315

390959BV00001B/2/P